MEDITATIONS FOR LENT

JAMES G. KIRK

The Westminster Press
Philadelphia

Book design by Gene Harris

First edition

Published by The Westminster Press®
Philadelphia, Pennsylvania

PRINTED IN THE UNITED STATES OF AMERICA

9 8 7 6 5 4 3 2 1

Library of Congress Cataloging-in-Publication Data

Kirk, James G.
  Meditations for Lent.

  Includes index.
  1. Lent—Meditations.   I. Title.
BV85.K55   1988   242'.34   88-17117
ISBN 0-664-25038-6 (pbk.)

MEDITATIONS
FOR LENT

BOOKS BY JAMES G. KIRK

Published by The Westminster Press

Meditations for Lent

Published by The Geneva Press

When We Gather:
A Book of Prayers for Worship
Year A   Year B   Year C

To my sons,

John G. and James K.,

who live life to the fullest

and soar among lofty heights

CONTENTS

Foreword   11

Ash Wednesday
   Endurance   *Hebrews 12:1-14*   17

Thursday
   Perfection   *Philippians 3:12-21*   19

Friday
   Forbearance   *Philippians 4:1-9*   21

Saturday
   Mercy   *Ezekiel 39:21-29*   23

FIRST WEEK

Sunday
   Pioneer   *Hebrews 2:10-18*   27

Monday
   Wilderness   *Mark 1:1-13*   30

Tuesday
   Fishing   *Mark 1:14-28*   33

Wednesday
   Touch   *Mark 1:29-45*   36

Thursday
   Forgiveness   *Mark 2:1-12*   39

Friday
  Humor   *1 Corinthians 3:16-23*   42

Saturday
  Sabbath   *Mark 2:23–3:6*   45

SECOND WEEK

Sunday
  Works   *John 5:19-24*   51

Monday
  Saints   *1 Corinthians 4:8-20*   54

Tuesday
  Leaven   *1 Corinthians 5:1-8*   57

Wednesay
  Hearing   *Mark 4:1-20*   60

Thursday
  Kingdom   *Mark 4:21-34*   63

Friday
  Turbulence   *Mark 4:35-41*   66

Saturday
  Sin   *Mark 5:1-20*   69

THIRD WEEK

Sunday
  Judgment   *John 5:25-29*   75

Monday
  Fair   *Mark 5:21-43*   78

Tuesday
  Dust   *Mark 6:1-13*   81

Wednesday
  Vengeance   *Mark 6:14-29*   84

Thursday
  Care-giving   *Mark 6:30-46*   87

Friday
  Expectations   *Mark 6:47-56*   90

Saturday
  Hypocrisy   *Mark 7:1-23*   93

FOURTH WEEK

Sunday
  Hunger and Thirst   *John 6:27-40*   99

Monday
  Bread   *1 Corinthians 10:14–11:1*   102

Tuesday
  Compassion   *Mark 8:1-10*   105

Wednesday
  Sight   *Mark 8:11-26*   108

Thursday
  Denial   *Mark 8:27–9:1*   111

Friday
  Transfiguration   *Mark 9:2-13*   114

Saturday
  Prayer, Fasting, and Almsgiving
    Mark 9:14-29   117

FIFTH WEEK

Sunday
  Stones   *John 8:46-59*   123

Monday
  Servant   *Mark 9:30-41*   126

Tuesday
  Salt   *Mark 9:42-50*   129

Wednesday
  Union *Mark 10:1-16*   132

Thursday
  Treasures *Mark 10:17-31*   135

Friday
  Baptism *Mark 10:32-45*   138

Saturday
  Well-being *Mark 10:46-52*   141

HOLY WEEK

Palm/Passion Sunday
  Peace *Zechariah 9:9-12*   147

Monday
  Prayer *Mark 11:12-25*   150

Tuesday
  Authority *Mark 11:27-33*   153

Wednesday
  Blessed *Mark 11:1-11*   156

Maundy Thursday
  Basin and Towel *Mark 14:12-25*   159

Good Friday
  No *John 13:36-38*   161

Holy Saturday
  Complete *Hebrews 4:1-16*   164

EASTER

Easter Sunday
  The Companion *Luke 24:13-35*   169

Index of Scripture Readings   173

FOREWORD

Lent is traditionally a time for spiritual discipline, a time to reflect on the maturity of our faith and what it might take to make us stronger Christians. The following meditations were written to assist the reader in that process. I chose, as a scriptural guide, daily Bible readings found in Supplemental Liturgical Resource 5, *Daily Prayer* (Westminster Press, 1987).

Each day's reading is meant to be a coordinated unit. The first paragraph highlights what is found in the scriptural passage. A theme was chosen unique to the passage and then developed as a thought for the day. The thoughts are meant to generate reflection throughout the day, both as to what the Bible says and how that message applies to our lives. A prayer concludes the day's meditation. The prayer is intended to be suggestive, and the reader may want to add her or his own thoughts. Notice, however, that all the prayers use the plural pronouns. That was intentional, since it is the writer's belief that even when we pray alone, our prayers are joined with and on behalf of the church universal.

Most of the Bible readings are from Mark. Again, that was intentional. Mark, as the shortest and most concise of the Gospels, provides the broadest overview of Jesus' ministry in a short space of time. I chose to cover as much of one Gospel as I could in a sequential manner, rather than using a variety of texts in a more random fashion. Again, Year Two of the daily lectionary provided that kind of framework.

Now, a word or two about the themes you will find throughout Lent. Jesus' baptism by John plays a significant role, as does his testing in the wilderness and subsequent preaching of the gospel. Those who follow Jesus are to repent of their past, their sins are forgiven, and the Holy Spirit will sustain them when they are tested. To be Jesus' disciple demands endurance and sacrifice, but such discipline always occurs in light of God's mercy and grace. There is throughout scripture the abundant affirmation that God will provide strength sufficient for each day's events.

Second, there is much to learn. Jesus spent time with his disciples teaching them and interpreting for them his acts of healing and what God's will implied. There is both anger and pathos in Jesus' message. He was angry with the religious authorities, particularly when they questioned his authority. He became frustrated with the disciples and their seeming lack of understanding for his mission. But, on the other hand, he lamented when his followers and others suffered. He sought to protect them from harm, to support and nurture them. Discipleship involves all of us in constantly learning how to correct and console at the same time.

Third, Lent is a time to sharpen the senses. Jesus himself spent time in the wilderness. He sensed the afflictions of those about him. He sought to heighten his disciples' awareness of God's benevolence in providing abundantly throughout the creation. Lent is a wonderful time for all of us to anticipate God's springtime. There are the sights and smells of spring as the days grow longer and blooms appear. As we anticipate the new life inherent in Easter, we also become more sensitive to the needs of others about us.

No book is written alone. While I take full responsibility for the thoughts contained in the meditations, I have received abundant inspiration and encouragement from those about me. The book is dedicated to sons John and Jamie. They called periodically just to check on its progress and how Dad was doing. My wife, Elizabeth, was always there to read a particular day's offering and to make suggestions on how it could be improved.

Two people are worthy of particular mention. Gladys Sargent, my administrative assistant, typed and proofed each page and took on the entire project as though it were her own. She was an invaluable partner throughout the entire endeavor and provided the constant affirmation to see it completed. Mildred Borton of Kalamazoo, Michigan, is one of those saints of the church who lives the Christian faith. She provided inspiration at just the right moments and was always available to celebrate a thought. To them, and to all the saints of Central Presbyterian Church, in Lafayette, Indiana, who surrounded me with their care and nurture, I say, Thanks be to God.

Easter 1988   J.G.K.

Hebrews 12:1-14   **Ash Wednesday**

ENDURANCE

The emphasis is on Jesus as the pioneer and perfecter of our faith. He sets the tone for that faith, as throughout his earthly life he endured whatever hostility was necessary in order that God's will would be fulfilled. Now he sits at God's right hand, there to intercede on our behalf, as through discipline we seek to be worthy of his call to "come, follow me!"

One of the most refreshing facts of the Christian faith is that we are not asked to respond in any supernatural way to Jesus Christ. Rather, we are asked to be quite human about it all. After all, it is God who in Christ accepts us as we are, who puts our lives right and shows us a better way. The clues we get on how to live that better way come from our belief that Jesus was very human indeed. He suffered more than most of us will ever be expected to endure. Yet he remained steadfast to God throughout whatever occurred.

This is why, when the word "endurance" is mentioned, we have a model to follow. We are asked nothing more than what our Savior himself practiced. Oh, but there is something else involved in endurance. It is this: Because Jesus himself learned to endure, he now intercedes on our behalf, so that we ourselves may find help to endure. In that respect, Jesus is like a coach; he stands beside us throughout our trials; he guides us in what steps to take; he knows how badly it hurts when we fall; he urges us onward as we seek to succeed.

There is no way that endurance just happens or that it occurs automatically in faith. There needs to be some toning of the faith muscles, a great deal of patience, and some concentrated exercise—all of which implies concentrated discipline and commitment over and over again.

The result, Paul reminds us, is that "endurance produces character, and character produces hope, and hope does not disappoint us" (Rom. 5:4–5). Why? because God's love has been poured into our hearts through the Holy Spirit, the same Spirit who bears witness to Jesus Christ, who endured the cross so that we may live as the humans God created us to be.

Most gracious God, who came that we might have life, and that indeed abundantly, we come with thanksgiving for Jesus, the pioneer and perfecter of our faith. As he went before us to show us your way, may we be bold to follow his teachings throughout the course of this day. As he now sits at God's right hand to intercede for us, may we confess our sins with assurance of your mercy and grace. Grant us the endurance to suffer whatever trials await us, that we may learn what it means to hope in your love which never fails.

Philippians 3:12-21 **Thursday**

PERFECTION

Paul's quest is to live by the power of Christ's resurrection. Not that he has already attained it, but he seeks to make the power his own, since Christ has made him his own. The alternative is those who live for the moment with its fleeting desires. Their problem is that they are never satisfied; cravings simply multiply, and satisfaction is fleeting. So Paul's admonition is to yearn for that power that can sustain life under all circumstances.

Perfection throughout the New Testament stands betwixt and between—betwixt what God has already accomplished and between what is yet to occur. As one writer reminds us, perfection is a matter of how you add up to seven: $6 + 1$ or $1 + 6$. For those who add $6 + 1$ there is constant striving through six days of work to attain the point when they can rest from their labors. They emphasize their accomplishments and take great joy in their pursuits. Their days are spent justifying their actions, and time is of the essence.

Those who add $1 + 6$ orient all they do by what God has already done on their behalf. They live in thanksgiving for God's mercy and grace, which surround, sustain, and uphold them. Life is a gift to be cherished, and accomplishments are to God's glory and honor.

Many of us probably fall into the $4 + 3$ or $5 + 2$ categories, sometimes well aware of how God watches over us, yet also driven by the pressures that surround us. Perfection is the ability to live betwixt and between the complete but not-yet-finished reality of God's all-embracing care for the creation. It really is a matter of learning to add up to seven by

1 + 6. For as you read the creation narrative, you hear how God saw all that God created and it was good; it was complete. Then God rested. Elsewhere in scripture we are invited to enter that rest, to live in light of the 1, or, as Paul writes, "Let us hold true to what we have attained" (v. 16).

As we do so, we will recognize how God is constantly present throughout the 6, or the not-yet-finished portion of our equation. "I press on toward the goal for the prize of the upward call of God in Christ Jesus" (v. 14). God then really is the author and finisher of our faith. Let us seek to live in light of that perfection, betwixt and between the complete but not-yet-finished power of Christ's resurrection.

You are the Author and Finisher of our faith, and we praise you for sustaining us throughout our past and for promising us your abiding love forevermore. Grant that our days may be lived in the glory of your love for us and that all we do will honor and praise your name. Throughout this day frustrate our endeavors that are not in accord with your will for us and enhance those efforts that reflect your desires. We press on toward the goal as Jesus Christ has made us his own.

Philippians 4:1-9   Friday

FORBEARANCE

Paul strikes the chord to rejoice in the Lord.
Through prayer and supplication, make your requests known to God. Surround your prayers at all
times with praise and thanksgiving for God's mercy
and grace. Lead godly lives and seek to enhance
whatever is honorable, pure, just, and lovely. Those
about you will recognize your good works and praise
God's name.

Jesus said, "Come to me, all who labor and are
heavy laden, and I will give you rest. Take my yoke
upon you, and learn from me" (Matt. 11:28–29). In
the Galatian letter Paul writes, "Bear one another's
burdens, and so fulfil the law of Christ" (Gal. 6:2).
Forbearance implies three things: Have patience, live
the question, and love your way into the answer.

One writer has said that we must have patience
with everything unresolved in our hearts and not
search for answers that could not be given at the
moment, because we would not be able to live them.
Patience is a positive virtue, resignation is not. Patience is admitting that things are not as they should
be, but we can wait. Patience implies doing whatever
is necessary to get where you want to be. That is the
difference between patience and resignation. Patience means to settle for the moment until what is
sought can occur; resignation is to do nothing to
bring it about. Forbearance implies patience, not resignation.

The television show *Jeopardy* has taught us an important lesson: How to ask the right question. Life
may just be an accumulation of answers, the trick to
which is learning how to live the questions. The
process is reversed so often, we are anxious because

we don't have all the answers. But if Christ is the answer, then perhaps we need to focus more on learning the questions. Prayer will then become the process of helping us to ask the appropriate questions. If God knows what we need before we ask it, maybe we ought to spend more time finding out what we need.

Then love your way into the answer by taking Christ's yoke upon you. Love your way into the answer as you bind yourself with your neighbor. Love your way into the answer through your willingness to suffer with Christ so that you may also be glorified with him. Love your way into the answer by resolving to do whatever will make a difference, whether it be in your own or your neighbor's life. As you take Christ's yoke upon you, cast your anxieties on God and free yourself to love your neighbor. Then all those about you will know your forbearance and praise God's name.

Merciful God, you know of our needs before this prayer leaves our lips, and we give you all praise for your compassionate care. You cradle us in your arms and hold our lives in the palm of your hand. Lift from our shoulders those burdens that today dwell heavily upon us. Grant to us patience as well as determination, courage for our quest as well as longing for your will, and care of our neighbors to match Christ's gift of sustaining grace.

Ezekiel 39:21-29   **Saturday**

MERCY

God's mercy surrounds Israel, which has felt the fury of divine judgment. The forecast is that they will dwell securely in the land, their transgressions forgiven and their fortunes restored. God's face will no longer be hidden from them; they will know God and be known as God's chosen people. God scatters those who transgress the divine will but gathers those who are deemed worthy of grace.

God's mercy is like a warm shower flowing over your body, washing away the suds used to cleanse you of the day's busyness. It is no wonder that water is used so much throughout scripture as a sign of God's mercy. Flowing water, the waters of our baptism, cool streams, wells of fresh water, the receding waters of the flood that engulfed Noah—all have throughout the ages reminded pilgrims of faith that they journey through life surrounded by signs of God's mercy.

Those who have committed some treacherous deed that has disappointed their friends and loved ones know what it means to live by God's mercy. Through time they rebuild relationships and regain the trust of those who remained faithful to them. Mercifully, in time the past is forgotten and the hope of the future makes the present once again bearable.

Those who have undergone surgery know what it means to live by God's mercy. They have committed their lives to the skilled medical team who will administer the anesthetic, perform the surgery, and support their vital functions until they reawaken and begin the process of recuperation and convalescence. They have throughout their deep sleep been mercifully sustained by those committed to their well-being.

Those who have been imprisoned by pervasive doubts of their self-worth know what it means to live by God's mercy. A glimmer of hope occurs when they receive a compliment, or the slightest word of encouragement, that allows them to put one foot in front of the other. Mercifully they begin to take those first halting steps with confidence that they will not always stumble and fall.

All of us who awaken from sleep to greet a new day know what it means to live by God's mercy. The resurrection to new life promised by Jesus comes with the dawn. Notice how the birds always start to sing before the sun arises. They are the first of all creatures to herald God's love and mercy, which will surround us throughout the day. From morning till evening and during the night's passage, God gathers us all in that merciful embrace which is so enduring.

Merciful God, who can withstand the force of your anger? Yet, through Christ you lift our drooping hands, strengthen our weak knees and make straight paths for our feet. We can walk henceforth with assurance that you will uphold us as we seek to be faithful. Grant that this day may be bathed in the glory of your abiding presence and that all we do may be deemed worthy of your grace.

FIRST WEEK

PIONEER

The author of the Letter to the Hebrews refers to Jesus as the pioneer of salvation and then goes on to describe why he was such. Jesus partook of the same nature as God's children: He suffered death on their behalf in order to deliver them from lifelong bondage; he was tempted in order to help those who followed; he was made like them in every respect in order to be a merciful and faithful high priest in God's service on their behalf.

In fact, Hebrews is the only place in scripture where Jesus is referred to as the "pioneer"; he is the pioneer of salvation and the pioneer of our faith (Heb. 12:2). On the one hand, Jesus is the source of our salvation; on the other, he goes before us to show us the way. Hebrews describes Jesus as opening the gates of heaven and providing access to the throne of God. Even now Christ sits at God's right hand to intercede on our behalf. We have then in Christ an advocate before the Judge in heaven, one who is familiar with our plight, who can sympathize with our condition, and who will make an appeal on our behalf.

Jesus goes before us to show us the way. In that sense, too, he is the pioneer of our faith. He has been called the "pathfinder"; elsewhere we read of him as "the way, and the truth, and the life." All the descriptions are similar. He blazed the trail of our journey in faith and showed us the way of salvation. The author of Hebrews in that sense could exhort the readers: "Let us run with perseverance the race that is set before us, looking to Jesus . . . , who for the joy that was set before him endured the cross" (Heb. 12:1–2). Jesus stood before the uncertainty of his

impending death, repudiated the possibility of un-
belief, and lived by confidence in the future.

There are four discernible themes associated with
Jesus as the pioneer and perfecter of our faith. First,
he is the source of encouragement and hope. He
came as one of us and himself pursued the journey
of faith. He was subjected to the ways of the world,
the likes of which many of us may never encounter.
He was cast into the wilderness, where he was
tempted and his commitment tried. When he taught,
his every word was scrutinized by the political and
religious authorities of his day. He sustained their
criticism and prevailed against all opposition.

Second, he suffered. Through him God disclosed
suffering as the way to glory. Gone are any false
notions of faith as a guarantee that life will be easy
and there will be no pain. Jesus led the way with the
cross he carried, and throughout scripture he ele-
vated the shame of the cross to a position of honor,
which all those who followed him would be expected to experience. Henceforth it would be during
the painful times of life that God would be most
present and Jesus our most constant companion.

Third, he inaugurated a community about him.
Jesus was gregarious, and those who followed him
were drawn into community with one another. That
is why the Lord's Supper is so important. It is just a
common meal, yet out of our breaking the bread and
drinking the cup, we gain trust, hope, and confidence
that we will share the same fate with the one who
went before us. We shall dine with him in glory.

Fourth, Jesus triumphed on our behalf. That
which none of us could or can do by ourselves—
namely, save ourselves from sin—Jesus accomplished for us. That fact brings us back to Jesus as the
author of our salvation. He broke the power of sin
and evil over us once and for all. In so doing, he freed

us to believe and hope in the good news that we are set free from bondage and are alive in Christ!

O God of our deliverance, we thank you for Jesus, the pioneer and perfecter of our faith. He is the author of salvation, source of our comfort, our guide and companion through life. Whatever occurs he will be there to sustain us, uplift us, and guide us. We give thanks that we need never walk alone, because he trod this earthly way before us and now sits at your right hand to intercede on our behalf.

WILDERNESS

John appears in the wilderness and foretells the coming of the one who would baptize with the Holy Spirit. As Jesus is baptized, the heavens open and the Spirit descends upon him. After hearing that he was the beloved Son with whom God was pleased, Jesus was driven into the wilderness, there to spend forty days. The angels ministered to him as the wilderness became his testing ground. His faith would teach others commitment, discipline, and perseverance.

The wilderness is often portrayed as a godforsaken tract of real estate not fit for beast or human. Yet we hear differently throughout scripture. As the Israelites journeyed through the wilderness, God was with them. God fed them and led them and taught them what it meant to obey. As Jesus encountered his time apart from the crowds, the angels ministered to him. God promised throughout history not to forsake the creation. Testimony abounds to the truth of that promise.

The wilderness conjures up images of aimless wandering, of people unable to get their bearings, with no identifiable landmarks upon which to fasten their attention. As time goes by, doubt occurs about any way to escape; hopelessness sets in and, with it, depression. Often persons ask, Why did this happen to me?

Wilderness wanderings aren't the first choice for many people's vacation plans. They would prefer to journey with their companions and to know where they are going, what pitfalls to expect, where the dangers are, and how long the trip should last. If their choice is the wilderness they want to know what guides to choose, which maps to buy, where to get the necessary provisions, how long the proper preparation should take. In other words, they want to be prepared.

There is no doubt that wilderness wanderings occasion the unexpected. They need not be aimless. The terrain may be unusual, but it is identifiable. The trek may seem interminable, but there can be limits. It might be a good idea to view the wilderness as those times and places when the best someone can do is to trust God completely. Defenses are down. People feel vulnerable; they no longer control their own destiny. It may be a time to rely on God, and sometimes God alone, to guide us. A time when the best we can do is put one foot in front of the other, because beyond that assurance the way may be precarious or even unknown.

Maybe that is why the wilderness is so often depicted as the testing ground for faith. During those wanderings, God for a time has the people dependent, attentive, humble, obedient, and hopeful. At other times God has to go to extremes just to get our attention. Even if it is a test, remember the petition in the Lord's Prayer which prays, "Lead us not into temptation." That petition asks God not to test people beyond their capacity to cope. Remember, God won't forsake the creation. Maybe the wilderness is similar to Nietzsche's words, "You must carry a chaos within you to give birth to a dancing star."

O God, you brought order from chaos and promised the creation that you would never forsake it; help us to order our lives that we do not forsake you. Accompany us through the perilous journeys of whatever wilderness awaits us and guide us by your Holy Spirit to repent of our sin. Ignite anew the flame of our faith so that we may become a consuming witness to the truth that in Christ we may weather whatever confronts us. Christ is living indeed!

Mark 1:14-28   **First Week: Tuesday**

FISHING

Jesus proclaims that the time is fulfilled, "Repent and believe in the gospel." He then goes in search of those who would follow him. The first four he finds are fishermen: Simon, Andrew, James, and John. He will make them fishers of women and men. The people soon found that Jesus taught with authority, an authority sufficient to command unclean spirits and to heal persons of whatever afflicted them. This was a person, indeed, with whom to be reckoned.

Izaak Walton, in his seventeenth-century classic *The Compleat Angler,* was convinced that fishing was an outward sign of inward grace, an expression of virtually religious identity with nature. Walton believed that Jesus knew what he was doing when he called the fishermen. These men were fitted for contemplation, and that is why Jesus chose three of them, Simon Peter, James, and John, to accompany him at his transfiguration. The fact that Jesus went looking for his disciples after his resurrection and found them preparing for a fish barbecue on the beach only proves Walton's point: Fishing is an outward sign of inward grace.

Fishing takes patience. Those who fish must wait patiently once the line hits the water. Any amount of anger, irritation, or frustration is only going to traverse itself along the line and onto the leader. Somehow the wary fish will know that something is amiss and shy away from what could have been a healthy strike. As Walton describes those who fish, they are of "mild, and sweet, and peaceable spirits." The first lesson of fishing is to cultivate the mild manner that will bring patience to wait upon the Lord.

Fishing takes practice, practice to learn the fine art of casting. How many times has a cast been made, only to have the hook get caught in a bush or behind a rock. No manner of power will dislodge the snag. Often what happens is that the power that was going to transport the hook cleanly into the water gets diverted into building a bird's nest of hook, leader, and line that ends up a mess ten feet in front of you. Expect the entanglements. Through practice they will occur less often.

Fishing takes perseverance. Those who fish will learn the condition of the water; they will acquaint themselves with what the fish are feeding on; they know where to expect them and when; they even try to think like the fish. Watch someone fishing, and you will see how it takes cast upon cast, trying one spot after another, changing one lure to another— the persistence to do whatever is necessary to get the strike that is sought.

Suddenly, you will make contact with the magic current of the world. You will learn how to throw enough line into the rod to reduce the voltage and ease the shock of what strikes. Electrical sparks will seem to be everywhere, for you have entered the life in the Spirit and have gone fishing with Christ. "Follow me and I will make you fishers of women and men."

O God, you commanded the waters to bring forth living creatures abundantly, and the element upon which your Spirit did first move; may the waters of our baptism continue to renew and refresh us. Help us to learn the patience, practice, and perseverance necessary to follow Christ's call to become fishers of women and men. May we be given the Spirit of guidance to grow as disciples, the counsel and might to be faithful and true. Guide us in the way that will lead others to know you more clearly and love you more dearly. Throughout the day let us worship you in thought, word, and deed.

Mark 1:29-45   **First Week: Wednesday**

TOUCH

Jesus embarks on a ministry of healing. The crowds surround him. He cures those with fever; he frees those afflicted with demons and makes clean the lepers. In the midst of it all, Jesus does something very human; he goes off by himself early one morning to pray. Suddenly, we catch a personal glimpse of the one we call Christ and Savior. Jesus sought God's guidance just as we want to do!

"Reach out and touch someone" has become a household phrase. Marketed by the phone company, its intention is for people to pick up their phones and call a friend or loved one. However, it has far deeper implications for those of us in the church. Touch was the keystone of Jesus' mission, the epitome of his healing ministry. He lifted those who could not walk; he put his hands on the blind and they could see; he cast out demons and rendered them mute; he touched lepers, cleansed them, and made them whole. When Peter and John had no silver and gold to give the lame man outside the temple, they gave him what they had: their hand in the name of Jesus Christ of Nazareth. The man walked into the temple praising God.

On the ceiling of the Sistine Chapel, Michelangelo captures the magnetism of God's reaching out to humankind. The sparks seem to fly across the slim gap that separates the two fingers from touching. One is almost tempted to ask the question, What would happen if the two fingers were to touch? Yet that is not our concern. Our concern is to be about the task Christ has called us to perform. What will happen when we reach out and touch our neighbor?

Touch is similar to the gap in spark plugs. The gap has to be set correctly so that there is sufficient spark to ignite the gas that drives the engine. Maybe that is why Michelangelo left the gap between God's and humankind's fingers. Our task is to fill the gap.

We are to provide the touch that unites God with our neighbors; our task is to provide the spark that will ignite their lives. That was what Jesus was teaching his disciples, and now we are to do it as we follow Christ's will.

Sometimes the touch will be one of consolation. We hear people say, "Just give me a hug." As we hold them we feel the energy that passes from one person to another and gives them strength to endure their burdens. Other times the touch may be a long-term commitment. "Take my hand," at those times, is their invitation to journey with them through a time in their lives. We need to be ready to make the commitment, because it will mean sharing with them their disappointments as well as their satisfactions. There will be those times when the touch needs to be more forceful, to correct wrongs or to keep people from destroying themselves. At those times we need a great deal of energy ourselves, for these can be very draining experiences. That is why Jesus kept those times to be with his God. If he were going to be in the gap between God's finger and humankind's finger, he knew that his energy would have to come from God. Jesus wanted to keep in touch. We need to do the same!

O God, you loved the world so much that you sent your only Son; we thank you for Jesus. He went about healing those who were afflicted. Throughout history his teachings have touched countless lives, our own included; he has laid his hands on our shoulders and asked us to follow him, the ministry to which he has called us. Make us worthy servants this day as we seek to be faithful. As we reach out to others, may our touch bring healing, vitality, and new hope to their lives.

FORGIVENESS

Jesus is teaching in a crowded room when down comes a pallet on which lies a paralytic. Jesus marvels at the faith of the paralytic's friends. Today, we would say they were tenacious. When Jesus forgave the paralytic's sins, a discussion arose among the onlookers: Who has authority to forgive sins besides God? Jesus knew where his authority came from and was frankly not afraid to answer them. The result: The paralytic walked and the crowd was amazed!

Week after week we hear in worship, "Friends, believe the good news of the Gospel; in Jesus Christ we are forgiven." The past is over and done. With the assurance of the new life which Jesus proclaimed, we are freed to face the future cleansed of our sin. It is an assurance worth repeating. Daily, we err and fall short of God's glory. Scripture assures us that Jesus Christ, who sits at God's right hand, intercedes on our behalf in spite of our shortcomings. So pastors remind us, as we humbly confess our sins, that God is merciful and just, and through Christ we hear again and again, "We are forgiven."

Likewise, the Lord's Prayer reminds us to "forgive us our debts as we forgive our debtors." God's forgiveness is unconditional and freely given. We, in turn, are to show the same merciful behavior toward our neighbors. Throughout the church's history it has been known as "passing the peace." Before going to the Lord's Table and partaking of the bread and grape of Christ's reconciliation, believers are to make peace with their enemies. Whatever the cause of their alienation from one another, Christ's table announces the dawn of a new era. Believers will come from north and south, east and west, and sit at table as God's reconciled people. This is a radical idea with far-reaching implications!

One implication is healing. Forgiveness does not just occur verbally. It involves restoring the person to wholeness. That is why Jesus could not simply leave the paralytic with the words, "Your sins are forgiven." The paralytic also needed to be able to walk out of the room. Forgiveness involves taking the time to allow other persons to walk again, time that will restore their dignity and allow them to retain a sense of integrity. It means doing whatever is necessary to let the wound drain and begin the slow process of healing without superficial scabs that keep the flesh raw beneath.

Another implication is the ability to forgive yourself. So often, you hear the comment, "I don't get mad, I get even." That kind of statement is like a dormant volcano seething with heat that someday will explode. People hold grudges that continue to fester and poison relationships. A crucial step toward healing is self-forgiveness. We cannot truly practice God's forgiveness of us unless we are able to forgive ourselves. Nor can we unburden ourselves of our grudges until we are truly at peace with ourselves. Then we can reach out to others and love our neighbors as ourselves.

A third implication of forgiveness is to take up our bed and walk rather than to rely on our crutches. A real temptation is constantly to live as a poor soul. Then we live dependent on our past failures, our nagging fears, and our constant regrets. The option is to do what the prodigal did: return to the embracing arms of your loving Parent and begin to build your life, which is already made whole by God's love in Christ.

Gracious God, forgive us our debts as we forgive our debtors. Help us to hear afresh the words that in Jesus Christ we are forgiven. May we reach out to those from whom we are estranged with courage and determination to bring healing. Help us this day to cast aside grudges that weigh heavily upon us and with renewed energy seek that peace with our neighbors which Christ came to proclaim. May we, too, be amazed by the wonders that are wrought when we obey Christ's commandment to love our neighbors as ourselves.

HUMOR

Paul's writing raises two points that are inter-related. The one is how we are God's temple and how God's Spirit dwells within us. In that sense we are to care for ourselves in such a way that God is glorified. The other has to do with the difference between wisdom and folly. This world's wisdom is folly in God's sight. Those who are fools for God's sake are wise. On the one hand God dwells within us, and on the other we have nothing to boast of, since we are Christ's; and Christ is God's.

One writer suggests that we should crown the clown with a capital *C*. The clown, according to Samuel Howard Miller, manages to extend the normal limits of our consciousness. We see in the clown's antics the contradictions that exist in all of us: dignity and embarrassment, pomp and rags, assurance and collapse, sentiment and sadness, innocence and guile. We are led by the clown's bold bluff only to crumple in public disaster.

The clown restores us to our true humanity and in that sense recovers for us a sense of salvation. We are shorn of unreal pomposity, the pretense of being invulnerable, and the delusion of being beyond it all. The clown helps us laugh at human foibles and puts our frailties right out there in public, where we can take a look at them. Suddenly, they don't loom large anymore. We see ourselves as others see us and as they see themselves, tripping over ourselves and able to laugh at our mistakes.

If the beginning of wisdom is the ability not to take ourselves too seriously, humor is the first lesson. The light side of life puts in perspective the very real truth that so much of what we do is serious business.

There is daily pain in living, and laughter is a medicine that can help us withstand the hurt. When visiting bereaved families, I have seen time and again how the memory of some humorous exploit in which the deceased engaged brought tears of laughter to the sorrowing family. There was catharsis in those tears, which blended into sorrowful joy. Laughter helped the family celebrate the truly human side of the life that had closed.

The Sunday comics should in that sense be seen as part of the day God has made; they help people rejoice and be glad. As you glance at the illustrations, it is easy to relate satire to situation and fable to fact. You rehearse through them your own confession of sin, only to emerge with laughter into the reality that you are forgiven. In a way the Sunday comics rehearse weekly Paul's message that this world's wisdom is folly in God's sight.

Christ was the epitome of the clown crowned with a capital *C*. How able he was to cut through the superficial seriousness with which the crowds surrounded themselves! He was led away by jeering mobs bent on their own phantasmagoria, hung on a cross in order to abate their own inability to deal with the love he sought to proclaim, and, when they thought they were free of him, he shows up on the beach at a morning's fish bake with the disciples! It is comforting at times to believe that God does have a sense of humor. Whether at the circus, during grief, in the comics, or rehearsing Christ's passion, God does have a way of putting our lives in perspective. Humor recovers for us a sense of salvation.

God of wisdom, God of mirth, God of gaiety, God of sorrows, we worship and adore you. You surround us in whatever condi-

tion we may find ourselves and support us all the day long. Guide us through whatever trials await us, and give us decency and strength to prevail. May all that we do this day enhance your kingdom among us, and may all our endeavors acclaim the Christ who dwells within.

SABBATH

The issue is the Sabbath and what laws the people should keep. Should the basics of life be maintained, such as eating and healing? The question comes down to this: For what purpose was the Sabbath set aside, for human obedience or to meet human needs? Clearly, Jesus preferred the latter interpretation. That got him in trouble throughout his ministry; he always put people ahead of codes of law, and his enemies plotted to destroy him.

The Sabbath was made for us; we weren't made for the Sabbath. Throughout history it has been a day set aside to give thanks, to rest, to restore the creation, to replenish the earth. It is all tied in with stewardship and what it means to be good stewards of God's gifts. In that sense, keeping the Sabbath has not so much to do with laws as it has to do with the question, What will it take to make you whole again?

Because of that, I think Jesus was quite correct in his response to the critics. His disciples were hungry when they picked grain on the Sabbath. The man's withered hand was of concern to him, and Jesus could restore him to wholeness. Legality wasn't the issue, restrictions distorted the truth. The truth of the matter was that Jesus was a responsible steward. His responsibility was to correct whatever imbalance there was and restore God's creatures to their intended goodness.

So the Sabbath has to do with restoration. It all goes back to the creation narrative itself, when we are told that God rested on the Sabbath. God worked with the creation for six days, saw that it was good, and rested. The creation was as God intended it to be. Responsibility for the care of that creation was then passed on to those who would dwell in the land. They were to be God's caretakers—or care-givers, as it turned out. They were to work the soil and till the ground; it would yield bountiful crops and fill the nations' storehouses. There would be abundance in the land, and God would be glorified. God saw that it was good.

You know as well as I do how centuries of human mismanagement have distorted that original intent. Nevertheless, our responsibility remains intact, our responsibility as stewards to care for God's creation. And that care should be the focus for all we do throughout the week. So we are brought back to the question asked some days ago: How do you add up to seven, 1 + 6 or 6 + 1? Jesus' use of the Sabbath would seem to imply the best answer is 1 + 6. That is to say, restoration was to be primary, rather than some laws that governed behavior. His concern was wholeness and whatever it took to achieve it. That quest conditioned his behavior weekly.

One more thing: If the Sabbath was made for us and we are Christ's, doesn't it make sense to be found among the members of Christ's body each Sabbath day? Where better can we find the restoration we need each week? How better can we learn what it means to be stewards of God's creation than among our companions as care-givers? What better way to enclose all we do throughout the week than by giving God thanks for the mercy and grace God gives us? Then it will always be comforting to hear, "Come to me, all who labor and are heavy laden, and I will give you rest" (Matt. 11:28).

O God, our God, how majestic is your name in all the earth!
I look at the heavens, the work of your fingers, the moon and stars

which you have established; what are we that you are mindful of us? Yet you have set us in the midst of your handiwork and given us dominion over it. Grant that our care may be to your glory and honor and make us responsible stewards. May we find rest from our labors in the wholeness Christ restores to us, and may we bring healing to others as he taught us to do.

SECOND WEEK

John 5:19-24   Second Week: Sunday

WORKS

John writes how Jesus taught his disciples that whatever the Father did the Son would do likewise. In that sense they were of one accord. Not only did the Father teach the Son, we read how the Son did the same things the Father did. To honor the Son was likewise to honor the Father, since both were one. The Father in turn would show the Son greater works he was doing. In that way, those who saw the Son could likewise marvel at the Father.

The Bible describes works in various ways. There are, of course, the works someone else teaches you. In scripture the rabbi was an important figure. Young men would work with the rabbi for as long as it took to accumulate the rabbi's knowledge. The student would be known by the reputation of the rabbi with whom he studied. We all have had our favorite teachers. And in some respects we have sought to emulate their teachings. We use their mannerisms, favorite sayings, and much of the behavior they taught us. So in that sense the works we do reflect those with whom we studied. Our works are their works, carried on to the next generation.

In another sense, works are not seen so favorably. Those are the works we boast of, as though we could somehow justify ourselves by what we do. Paul insisted that we are saved by faith and not by works. There is nothing we can do to redeem ourselves in God's sight. Only Christ could do that, and did so by God's grace in spite of us. So, Paul wrote, "Then what becomes of our boasting? It is excluded. On what principle? On the principle of works? No, but on the principle of faith" (Rom. 3:27). Elsewhere he wrote, "Let him who boasts, boast of the Lord" (1 Cor. 1:31). That is to say, no works we might do on our own could ever earn us the right to stand proudly before God's judgment seat. There would be no basis upon which to make a case for ourselves. That case could only be made by Christ, and it was made quite apart from anything we did to earn it.

A third type of works is mentioned in the letter of James. There we read, "You see that a man is justified by works and not by faith alone" (James 2:24). For James, what believers did would reflect what they believed. Accordingly, how they believed would determine what they did. So people could not say they believed in God and behave contrary to that conviction. John portrayed the same thought in his well-known passage, "If any one says, 'I love God,' and hates his brother, he is a liar; for he who does not love his brother whom he has seen, cannot love God whom he has not seen" (1 John 4:20). Faith in this sense was active in the works one performed. Works in that sense completed one's faith.

The fourth type of works were those described by Jesus, "I and the Father are one" (John 10:30). There John wanted to portray Jesus much the same way as the Nicene Creed was to portray him years later. We believe "in one Lord Jesus Christ, the only-begotten Son of God, . . . begotten, not made, being of one substance with the Father by whom all things were made." Whatever Jesus did was identical with God's will, and in that sense Jesus was truly Emmanuel, God with us.

We pray, "Not my will, but thine, be done." Let us reflect on the works we do throughout the course of the day. May we strive in all that we do to obey God's will for us, so that others will see our good works and glorify God who is in heaven.

"All glory, laud, and honor to thee, Redeemer, King. . . . Our praise and prayer and anthems before thee we present." We give thanks that in Christ thou hast seen fit to call us servants. May all that we do be pleasing in thy sight. Let the works of our hands, the words of our mouths, and the meditations of our hearts be a pleasing sacrifice of praise and thanksgiving to thee, our Rock and our Redeemer.

SAINTS

Paul writes to admonish the Christians in Corinth. He sets forth the terms of discipleship and urges them to imitate his behavior: When reviled, he blessed; when persecuted, he endured; when slandered, he tried to conciliate; he became as the refuse of the world. Why? to exhibit the power of God's kingdom in the world. Sent as God's saints into the world, they were to become fools for Christ's sake.

Leonard Cohen wrote that a saint is a person who has achieved a kind of balance amid the world's confusion. The energy needed to maintain that balance seems to derive from love—love for the world with all its uncertainties and hard realities. The saint does not change the world but rather moves freely in it, gloriously impervious to the forces that drag others down. The saint rides the snowdrifts like an escaped ski, caressing the hill, accepting out of love for the world the laws of gravity and chance.

The energy of love is to bless when reviled, to endure when persecuted, to conciliate when slandered, and thereby to exhibit the power of God's kingdom in the world. Such energy sets the world's ways topsy-turvy, so a balance results that can bring some order out of the chaos.

Saints do have a way of caressing the hills of life like an escaped ski. They are not afraid to take the downhill run propelled with a balance the Spirit of Christ provides them. The balance comes with their awareness of being loved by God, loved so much that God sent Christ into the world to set them free: free to become the creatures God created them to be, endowed with unique gifts and talents that set them apart from all the others, empowered to operate within the cosmos of God's energy and supreme design to right the wrongs and disorders they see about them.

Theirs is an abandon of sorts, for they care more about righting the universe than they do about their own grandeur. They will risk the mockery of the mobs; they will suffer abuse when others revile them and judge them according to worldly standards; they will not be afraid to stand alone on the windswept hills of life when others about them seek the safety of havens they secure for themselves. Saints believe that their stance will somehow bring order out of chaos.

Saints know that what they do will not dissolve the chaos. Arrogance is not within them. Rather, they are often called fools. They are fools for not going along with the crowd; they are fools for not making the system work for them; they are fools for not standing up for their rights; they are fools for not fighting back; they are fools for Christ.

The crowds may never understand the saints, but they will never be able to ignore them. Like escaped skis the saints will always appear. They will be there to show the crowds a better way. They will use the power invested by God, be it pen, ballot, proclamation, example, reason, sacrifice, or whatever means are appropriate as the energy of love exudes from their every pore, the energy sent from God, who so loved the world.

O God, you bring order out of chaos and set the creation aright through Christ's love and reconciliation. Create within us that burning desire to serve our neighbors, inflamed with the Holy

Spirit who guides and corrects us, and tempered by Christ's teachings in all that we do: May we this day and throughout the week bring a sense of balance to those affairs over which we have some control and set aright those beyond our grasp, through your loving and powerful embrace.

1 Corinthians 5:1-8   **Second Week: Tuesday**

LEAVEN

Paul attacks the immorality in the Corinthian community. It was widespread and damaging to the very fiber of their life together. As with old leaven, the people could not rise above their sins. What was needed was the unleavened bread of sincerity and truth. If they were truly to celebrate the new life inherent in Christ's sacrifice on their behalf, they would need to cleanse themselves of their old ways and be washed in the blood of the lamb.

I have this lump of sourdough that's over fifty years old. In many ways it's just like a member of the family. Weekly, it needs to be fed. When it's not used it can get diseased. It really is happiest when it's worked every day. In order to be used it needs to be at room temperature. When fed, the ingredients need to be warmed. You can't rush it when it is working but must allow it time, almost twice as much time as commercial yeast. Sourdough is a living, natural leaven, and in that respect it requires proper care and maintenance.

There are tricks to using commercial yeast as well. One that I learned some years ago was always to proof your yeast before you baked. Put the package of yeast in a bowl and add a teaspoon of sugar and warm water. The water needs to be just the right temperature, between 99 and 110 degrees Fahrenheit. Too cold, and the yeast won't work; too hot, and you will kill it. The best way to test the water is the same way you test a baby's bottle: If the liquid is warm but not too hot when drops fall on the skin, it is ready. The yeast will consume the sugar and begin to bubble if it is usable. If it doesn't proof, then you won't waste all the baking ingredients on worthless yeast.

Jesus taught that "the kingdom of heaven is like leaven which a woman took and hid in three measures of flour, till it was all leavened" (Matt. 13:33). Good, well-fed sourdough starter can permeate the dough and create the most pleasing aromas and truly wonderful-tasting breads. Commercial yeast will likewise cause the lump to come alive and make your bread light, porous, and even-textured.

For Paul, unfortunately, immorality had so permeated the people that their only solution was to rid themselves of all the old leaven and become like the unleavened bread of sincerity and truth. The promise of Jesus' kingdom was no longer alive in them; their malice and greed were spreading and infecting the whole.

Like sourdough starter, the kingdom of heaven needs to be worked daily in order for it to be most effective. Left idle, it will eventually become dormant within us and to restore its effects will take greater effort. With the proper care and nourishment it will be a lifelong companion.

As with commercial yeast, so with the kingdom; it will do no harm to proof it. Use it in daily decisions and watch the results. Your life will begin to take on the effects of being permeated with a new spirit, the Holy Spirit that cannot be contained. Then, when it comes to those major decisions all of us must make, that same Spirit will literally cause you to rise to the occasion.

"Our Father who art in heaven, hallowed be thy name. . . . Give us this day our daily bread." Sustain us with the nourishment necessary for us to overcome those temptations that

may turn us from your will for us. Help us to surpass our tendencies toward greed and malice, which inflict evil upon our neighbors. Restore within us the leaven of your kingdom, whereby in all our acts your name is praised and you receive the glory you are due.

Mark 4:1-20   **Second Week: Wednesday**

HEARING

Jesus begins to teach in parables. Perhaps one of his most famous is the parable of the seed that is sown. Birds ate the seed sown along the path. Some seed fell on rocky ground; it quickly sprouted and the sun scorched it. The seed among the thorns hadn't much chance. Only the seed that fell into good soil eventually yielded grain, and that indeed abundantly. Jesus concluded his teaching with, "Those who have ears to hear, let them hear."

How well do you hear what someone says to you? There is a difference between listening to someone and hearing what that person has to say. We have all heard of selective listening. People tune into what they want to hear and filter out what amounts to noise for which they have no use. Today's lesson is to hear what someone says.

Hearing takes discipline. Communication is an art that must be learned and practiced daily. To practice the art is to be aware of some of the blocks that keep communication from occurring. Along with selective listening, there is what could be called the "path block." The path block is used by those who are intent on going their own way. They pursue their own interests. When they engage in conversation they wait for the other person to stop talking, so they can say what they think is important. They seldom hear what another says. To them it is just so much noise; they wait for a break in the noise and will often interrupt if it continues. A popular comment used by path-block people is "Yes, but." The "but" indicates that what is important is about to follow. Words get eaten up in the process, and hearing does not occur.

"Rocky ground" listening is practiced by those

who only listen to those who agree with them. They pursue conversation in order to gain support and bolster their position. Like the seed that fell on rocky ground, there is no depth of commitment to what the other person is saying. Rather, there is a fleeting loyalty that will only last as long as the conversation is useful. Once the words have served their purpose, they fade quickly and eventually wither. Hearing occurs, but only in order to serve a purpose.

"Thorny" listening is a block commonly used in arguments. People who argue often have their minds already determined and their positions set. They are in no mood to be dissuaded from what they consider to be the facts. They will pursue the conversation only to weaken the other person's position: that is to say, to choke the opposition. In such cases the words often fly by one another, and neither party hears what the other says.

"Good soil" listening occurs when people are genuinely receptive to what someone says. They care about the other person and want to nourish her or his beliefs. They will provide an atmosphere whereby the other will feel accepted and cared for. They will be patient and give the other whatever time it takes. They may even repeat what the other said in order to gain clarification. There are no interruptions and seldom any distractions.

As you can imagine, "good soil" conversation takes a great deal of effort. It involves commitment. There needs to be a willingness to endure for however long it takes in order for the others to express themselves. That's why hearing takes discipline. Start slowly. A whole new world will open to you!

You are a compassionate God. You stoop to hear the faint whisper of your children. You sent Jesus as the Word who dwelt among us and who now intercedes for us. We give you thanks for his teachings. Let us have ears to hear what he proclaimed. May we truly listen to what our neighbors say to us. Give us commitment to nourish the soil of our own understanding. Let the seeds of their thoughts germinate into flowering relationships that produce allegiance, trust, and mutual growth.

Mark 4:21-34   Second Week: Thursday

KINGDOM

Jesus teaches about the kingdom of heaven. Let its light shine, he said. It also has to do with how you give to others. Seemingly, the more you give, the more you'll get in return. Hoard what you have, and eventually that will be taken from you. Of itself, the kingdom will grow within you; you will harvest its benefits daily. Do not be misled by its origins. As with the mustard seed, what is sown as the smallest may eventually become a haven for all who seek shelter.

Dear Jennifer:

I hope that by the time you read this letter you will understand better what happened to you last Sunday, when you were baptized. The reading from the Bible contained the parables Jesus taught about the kingdom of heaven. The minister called you a child of the covenant, said you were blessed, and invited you to claim your inheritance in God's kingdom.

When you were born, you inherited the right to breathe and to grow, the right to play and get into fights with your brother; you inherited your parents' love as well as their discipline, and the opportunity to learn and help others to learn; you inherited a wonderful country: fields and flowers, streams and mountains, oceans and parks, villages and huge cities that go on for miles. You inherited all these benefits as well as the problems. They were handed to you almost at the time you took your first breath in the hospital.

When water was splashed on you during the baptism, you inherited a lot more. It was as though we in the congregation said, "You need never walk through life alone, because we will be there to walk with you. Now you are a member of our family, too. We are the family of Jesus, and together we will rely on him to guide us." You inherited the teachings of Jesus as a guide to how to behave, how to make decisions, how to help other people, and how to trust in God in whatever you do. The congregation promised that day to stand beside you throughout life. I have seen some of those people cry when some of us were sad; I have seen a lot of them very happy when we were successful; I have seen them give money, time, and a lot of their influence to help others get ahead in life.

Some days you have probably thought that your room was your kingdom. From there you can launch great dreams of what you want to do with your life. There you're the boss. You like to think of it as your place, your bed, your toys, your clothes. When the world outside seemed pretty tough, you could always go to your room and things were better there. Your room was safe; it was base where no one could tag you out; it was your kingdom and you were the boss. You can't just stay in your room all day, though, as you know. Whenever you go out you are going to meet people in trouble, hear about nations at war. Some people can't get enough food to eat or clothes to wear or a place to live. Jesus wanted his disciples to care about those people because they also live in God's kingdom. You care about them, and for them also, because they are special, just as you are.

And Jennifer, daily remember your baptism. It was your initiation into God's kingdom. Remember that as the minister held you then, God continues to hold you day by day. As the water was poured over you, Christ continues to offer prayers to God on your behalf. As the congregation promised to care for you, God's Spirit embraces you this day. You will never walk alone, for you journey within God's kingdom.

Great and wonderful God, sovereign of all nations and prince of peace, we thank you that we may dwell as heirs of your kingdom. Make us fit inhabitants of your estate and worthy participants in your design for all of creation. Let your light shine through all we do, that others may give you all glory. Help us this day to remember our baptism. As we celebrate the past, rededicate us to the future with commitment and zeal as we follow the Christ.

TURBULENCE

Jesus goes for a boat ride. While he is asleep in the stern, a strong wind comes up and threatens to leave the boat awash. Jesus rebukes the wind and calms the seas. What type of person was this whom even the seas and winds obeyed? Jesus simply asked his companions what they feared. Had they no faith? The question is one that confronts us all during turbulent times.

David Mazel tells the story of Sadie Josephson. When she was seventy-five her husband died, leaving her with little insurance and an old house. Sadie decided to become a laundress, something she knew she could do well. Soon all her neighbors in Brooklyn preferred Sadie to the local laundromat. Even those with their own washers and dryers took their laundry to Sadie. She did everything by hand.

Sadie would go about the neighborhood and collect their wash in a little red wagon. Then she would pull it home, carry the wash to her basement, fill her tubs with steaming hot water, fetch her bar of yellow soap and her washboard, get down on her knees, and scrub away. When she was done washing she would wring each piece under the tap until it was soapless.

Up the stairs Sadie would go and out back of her house to the greenhouse. There, clotheslines were strung on which clothespins sat like birds at a convention. Sadie would hang the clothes until they were dry and then attack each piece with her iron until they contained not a wrinkle. When the laundry was folded and stacked it was time to load her red wagon for the return trip through the neighborhood.

David Mazel decided to save her that trip, so he went to pick up his laundry. He was filled with compassion for this seventy-five-year-old laundress. Why did she do such tedious labor? he asked her. Surely there was something less strenuous she could do. How could he help her, and what did she need to keep from spending her days like some hireling? In reply, Sadie told him her story.

"God gives me two candles, the candle of strength and the candle of hope. Some days the candle of strength is blown out and I only have the candle of hope. Other days the candle of hope is blown out and I have the candle of strength. God does not let both candles be out at the same time. Today, both candles are burning brightly, and from now on they always will." And with that she gave him his laundry and shooed him on his way.

Everyone endures turbulent times, times when the ship of life is battered by the angry waves and gusty winds. For Sadie it would have been easy to board up the windows of the house and spend her days in darkened rooms waiting for death to overtake her. She chose rather to spend her strength serving her neighbors, doing what she knew she could do well. Some days she only had hope to go on; other days she relied more on strength. The day she met David Mazel she was running on both.

During our turbulent times, we can trust that God will not let both candles be extinguished at once. We can pray daily that God will grant us sufficient strength to meet the challenges that await us. As Hebrews reminds us, "Faith is the assurance of things hoped for, the conviction of things not seen" (Heb. 11:1). So trust in God and hope in the Lord. God will provide.

You are the subject of awe and the source of wisdom, O God, as you still the turbulence within us and calm our troubled spirits. We thank you for the peace that passes all understanding and sets our minds at rest. Give to us strength to sustain us through the nights of our forebodings and help us to rise to the dawn with hope in your compassionate care for us. Leave us not alone, for we rely upon your embrace to uphold us, O God, our strength and shield.

SIN

Jesus encounters the Gerasene demoniac and cleanses him of his unclean spirits. When the crowds saw the demoniac sitting calmly and in his right mind they were alarmed and begged Jesus to depart from their neighborhood. Why? Were they afraid of his power? Did they fear Jesus might expose their demons as well? Jesus told the Gerasene to tell his people what the Lord had done. He, like all of us, now lived by God's mercy.

Whatever Became of Sin? That was the title of Karl Menninger's book, published in 1973. It's a good question. Whatever did become of sin? The confessions of the church are clear and uncompromising about original sin as a human predicament. The Second Helvetic Confession defines it clearly: "That innate corruption of man which has been derived or propagated in us all from our first parents, by which we, immersed in perverse desires and averse to all good, are inclined to all evil."

The Westminster Confession makes the classic statement that "our first parents . . . fell from their original righteousness and communion with God, and so became dead in sin, and wholly defiled." In sin, says the Confession of 1967, "men claim mastery of their own lives, turn against God and their fellow men, and become exploiters and despoilers of the world. . . . All men, good and bad alike, are in the wrong before God and helpless without his forgiveness."

"Perverse desires," "wholly defiled," "exploiters and despoilers of the world": It doesn't sound good, does it? Regardless of whatever became of sin, it sounds as though there is plenty of it around. The question is not whatever became of sin, the question is how do we deal with it?

One way we deal with it is to confess it, daily in our time of prayer and weekly in the corporate confession of sin we pray in worship. To confess our sin instills in each one of us a healthy and wholesome sense of guilt. Now, read again what I just wrote: a healthy and wholesome sense of guilt. Guilt in that sense is proof that God is not just playing with us. God took this life so seriously and took the creation so seriously that nothing must stand in God's way. God acted on that intention in Jesus' sacrificial death. Today God is just as serious about that commitment to the integrity and purpose of creation.

Anything that continues to stand in the way is going to withstand the purging wrath of God's anger. Those who continue to frustrate such a plan are going to be held accountable. If that instills in people a healthy and wholesome sense of guilt, so be it, because only with guilt does healing come. Guilt in that sense is like opening a wound and letting it drain. All the poison needs to seep out, or else it will continue to fester and contaminate the whole system.

So confess your sin, apply a compress to the open wound of your wrongs in God's sight. What will seep out is arrogance, pride, boasting, defensiveness, selfishness, unwillingness to deal with reality, immobility, fear, anger, and conceit. Those are the demons that afflict us. As they depart, we will be cleansed to hear the reconciling love of God in Jesus Christ and receive the fruits of the Spirit: love, joy, peace, patience, kindness, goodness, faithfulness, gentleness, and self-control.

Gracious God, you brought Christ into the world to bear our afflictions, and by his stripes we are healed; no come with thanksgiving for his cleansing redemption. Purge the stain of sin within us and give us clean hearts, that we may serve you more faithfully. Renew right minds that we may enjoy the fruits of your Spirit and abound in the love, joy, peace, goodness, and faithfulness we find in the reconciling love of Christ Jesus, our Savior and Lord.

THIRD WEEK

JUDGMENT

Jesus foretells the time when the dead will hear the voice of the Son of God. It will be a time of judgment. The tombs will open and the dead will come forth; the ones who have done well will receive the resurrection of life; those who have done evil will receive the resurrection of judgment. No time is allowed for plea bargaining; the time is up. The coming age is already present in Jesus; hear the good news of the Gospel!

How many times have you heard that someone acted on the basis of a "judgment call"? This implies that the person weighed all the facts and made a decision accordingly. She or he may have had good judgment or bad judgment, depending on the outcome. However, a decision had to be made, and, regardless of the outcome, the person acted in a decisive way.

John portrays Jesus as making a judgment call. All the facts are at hand. Jesus has come to reveal God's will to the people. "Those who have ears to hear, let them hear." No one can claim exemption. Even the dead will be held accountable. Those who are physically dead will find the gates of their tombs opened and their lives scrutinized on the basis of their obedience to God. Those who are spiritually dead will find their ears unplugged, and they will hear the voice of God's Son. What then? "Truly, truly, I say to you, he who hears my word and believes him who sent me, has eternal life; he does not come into judgment, but has passed from death to life" (John 5:24). For Jesus the judgment call throughout his life was the choice he offered: life or death.

Judgment had its origins in the very beginning of

life itself. According to the creation narrative, man and woman wanted the freedom to judge for themselves. God had planned for them to be completely obedient. But since they would have it otherwise, God determined that from then on they would be held accountable for their actions. So as a result, we have the freedom to make choices, but we are also given responsibility for the choices we make.

Daily we make countless judgments. Our quest as Christians has been to align those judgments as closely as possible with Christ's teachings. Jesus taught us to judge circumstances rather than people: "Do not judge by appearances, but judge with right judgment" (John 7:24). Paul wrote at length, urging his readers not to pass judgment on others but to understand the circumstances behind their behavior.

There is a difference between making judgments and being judgmental. Those who are judgmental assume that they are the judge of how someone else behaves. They have a tendency to categorize people or expect them to behave in certain ways. Often they don't give others the same freedom to decide that they claim for themselves. Paul asked the Roman church, "Why do you pass judgment on your brother? . . . For we shall all stand before the judgment seat of God" (Rom. 14:10).

On our behalf, Jesus Christ took upon himself God's judgment. In so doing, he freed all those who believe in him so that they can be assured of God's pardon. Paul implied that it would then be folly for believers to accuse others of offenses for which God in Christ has forgiven them. So the lesson becomes clear. All of us stand before God worthy of judgment, but in Christ we are forgiven. Let us not then be judgmental of others, but rather pursue peace with our sisters and brothers for the mutual upbuilding of all. Then, through Christ, we can together seek to make judgments that will give God honor and glory.

Holy God, who could withstand your judgment, who could endure your wrath? Yet in Christ you have assured us of pardon and cleansed us of sin. Make us worthy of your benevolence and help us to appreciate your care. Let us not be so quick to judge others, for fear that we ourselves be judged. Cast us not away from your mercy but surround us with grace, so that the judgments we make will prove worthy of Christ's sacrifice on our behalf.

FAIR

Jairus comes and asks Jesus to heal his daughter, who is about to die. On the way to Jairus's house a woman with a flow of blood for twelve years touches his garment. The hemorrhage ceases and she is healed. Jesus went into Jairus's house and told the girl to rise. She too was cured. She got up and walked. To the woman he said that her faith had made her well. He told the girl's parents to give her something to eat. In both cases life resumed after what could have been tragedy.

A divorced mother's son falls to his death just three days after he entered college. A competent forty-year-old executive woman suffers a stroke and is left with an inoperable blood clot wedged deep in her brain. A sixty-year-old widow is fired from her job and now faces the grim prospect of living off her $279 widow's payment from Social Security. A sixteen-year-old athletic boy loses his left leg due to bone cancer. Ugo Betti has written (in *Gambler,* Act 2), "To believe in God is to know that all the rules will be fair and that there will be wonderful surprises." What is fair?

"Fair" is not blaming God for whatever happens. God has throughout history been faithful, has repeatedly proved trustworthy. God did not sacrifice Jesus out of a lack of care for the creation. God cares enough to cry with us each time we shed a tear. God is as frustrated as we are when forces seem to afflict us. God ultimately wants what is good for us. God knows what pain we endure, because the son of God hung on the cross.

"Fair" is how persons respond to what has been

dealt them. Kenny Rogers, the country and western singer, has some homespun wisdom in his song "The Gambler." As any cardplayer will admit, it's how the hand is played that results in a win or a loss. And it is when the dealing is done that the score is known, not after just one or two hands.

"To believe in God is to know that all the rules will be fair and that there will be wonderful surprises." To believe in that sense is not just to surrender. To believe in God is to work as hard as is necessary to come to resolution about whatever is causing pain. To believe is to have the assurance that day by day God will grant strength sufficient for the day (not tomorrow or three weeks from now, but strength for today).

Fair in that sense will no longer be on our terms; it will be on God's terms. And in most cases we may not know from moment to moment what fair will be. Sometimes we think we know and set up our standards accordingly. Yet again, as Kenny Rogers reminds us, every hand's a winner, every hand's a loser. At those times we trust in God alone to guide us.

There will be wonderful surprises. Christians time and again are surprised when miracles occur, new life emerges, resolutions change what seemed inevitable, or problems fade away or are put in perspective. The Holy Spirit continues to hover about us. Christ continues to intercede for us when our sighs are too deep for words. What is fair? God is fair. God will provide for all our needs as we tend to the work God calls us to do.

Great God, your loyalty is constant and your love endures forever. You know of our needs before we utter them. You sur-

round us with your benevolent care and bounteous compassion. Guide us through perilous times. Give us encouragement to endure those trials that are before us. Help us to see your loving hands enfolding us. Yoke us with Christ, who suffered even the cross, that with mutual forbearance we can uphold all who are afflicted and sustain them with love.

Mark 6:1-13   Third Week: Tuesday

DUST

Jesus finds out how it feels when you go home again. The people did not treat him with respect, nor were they in any mood to follow his teachings. Rather, he was led to conclude that a prophet is not without honor except in his or her own country. He then sent out the disciples and told them, if they were not received well in a particular city, to shake the dust off their feet and move on.

Dust is everywhere: in the air, kicked up on dry days, a most pervasive part of everyday living. Fastidious homemakers see dust as a constant challenge. Dustcloth in hand, they attack it, only to have it settle again soon after they are done. Outside, no one can escape dust; it gets in your eyes and nose, clings to your body, soils the clothes, and must be removed. Dust is a fact of creation, an ever-constant reminder that God created humanity from the dust and that to dust all humanity shall return.

Dust in the scripture today may also be used as a metaphor to describe our discipleship. In that respect there could be three types of dust: consequential dust, which is the most pervasive; catastrophic dust, which occurs less often but must be dealt with; and neglected dust, dust that we allow to accumulate from disregard, thoughtlessness, indifference, or laziness.

Consequential dust is everywhere. It is a fact of the creation and a constant companion throughout the day. Most people pay no attention to it, since nothing can be done to avoid it; it is part of the air we breathe. To shake consequential dust off your feet is the same as not worrying about what you can't change. It is obvious that daily life carries with it certain burdens. Know and pay attention to what is important and shake off the rest. In that case, what Jesus told his disciples meant that if they were not treated well it didn't matter; move on!

Catastrophic dust occurs less often but must be dealt with. The eruption of Mount St. Helens on May 18, 1980, was an example of catastrophic dust. Devastation rained down for miles around, killing wildlife, forests, and people. The death or loss of a loved one is an example of catastrophic dust. The urn of ashes is a visible reminder of a catastrophe that has occurred and the grief that has followed.

Trevanian in his book *The Main* wrote, "Of course grief is good! The greatest proof that God is not just playing cruel games with us is that He gave us the ability to grieve, and to forget. When one is wounded—I don't mean physically—forgetfulness cauterizes and heals it over, but there would be rancor and hate and bitterness trapped under the scar. Grief is how you drain the wound so it doesn't poison you" (Harcourt Brace Jovanovich, 1976; p. 233). Wherever there is catastrophic dust you need to cleanse the wound; otherwise it will poison the system.

Neglected dust, if left long enough, causes a chemical reaction that mars the original surface. A film appears that will take treatment to remove. Pockmarks occur that may cause permanent damage, which might inhibit or prohibit complete restoration. Neglected dust is found in those areas we would just as soon forget, cannot be bothered with, or find difficult to attend to.

Sometimes faith gets neglected and people find it difficult to trust in Christ, or to practice love for their neighbors, or discipline themselves to pray daily, or to rely on God's grace for forgiveness, or to use their opportunities to worship. Faith may then lose its luster and become tarnished or dull. We need to hear Jesus tell us, "Shake off the dust that is on your feet" so that you can "come, follow me."

Most gracious and loving God, all praise be unto you. We thank you for the legacy of discipleship, the legions who have served you faithfully throughout the years. As Christ sent out disciples two by two, he now sends us out into the world. Gird us with the mantle of faithfulness and the breastplate of courage; make us bold in our ventures to serve him. Give us the confidence of your Spirit's abiding presence and guidance, that what we say and do may bring glory and honor to your precious name.

Mark 6:14-29   Third Week: Wednesday

VENGEANCE

The question arises of where Jesus' powers came from. Some said John the baptizer was alive in him. Herod wondered how that could be, since he had had John beheaded. For some time Herodias had borne a grudge against John because he disapproved of her marriage to Herod. Her daughter's dancing pleased Herod and provided the perfect opportunity for Herodias to get revenge. She got John's head delivered to her on a platter.

Let's come back to the notion of "I don't get mad, I get even." There are times when life just isn't fair. People feel they have been dealt a bad hand. During those times, they may seek revenge. Herodias sought it and got John's head. While most of us have never gone that far, let's think about the dynamics of vengeance. Why do some people not get mad, they just get even?

Usually people think about revenge when they're cornered. There don't seem to be other alternatives. When bad things happen to people they seek causes. Many fix the blame on something or someone. They blame inanimate objects such as the zodiac, the moon's fullness, the forces of evil, fate, even getting up on the wrong side of the bed. Luck is a common inanimate concept but some people personalize it; Lady Luck is then said to have smiled or frowned on them.

Blame can also can be fixed on animate objects. In such cases the forces of evil are assigned anthropomorphic attributes. Satan, demons, spirits, political parties, ideologies such as communism, particular races of people, bureaucracies, systems, or institutions may assume personalities. In time those animate forces are held accountable for much that is at work in society.

A second characteristic of vengeance is that it is all-consuming. Whether it be against a particular individual, a group of people, or an animate or inanimate object, eventually a grudge takes on a life of its own. It becomes like a cancer: It takes away time that would normally be spent on more productive pursuits; it destroys whatever peaceful tendencies the person otherwise entertains; it consumes inordinate amounts of energy, often with very negative results; it eliminates possibilities for seeking healthy resolutions to the conflict. Eventually it may even destroy the person.

Third, vengeance hinders or even eliminates any possibility of reconciliation. Herodias got what she wanted, but it took John's death to satisfy her. Herod, although he finally capitulated, tried at first to protect John and imprisoned him. Only reluctantly did he agree to her wishes, and that was through the wiles of her daughter. There was no possibility of time's eliminating the cause of her grudge. In that case, vengeance destroyed John.

Vengeance does not seem to have any redeeming qualities. It makes inanimate and animate causes the objects of fixation in order to blame something, it can consume the person holding a grudge, or it may even destroy the person against whom a grudge is held. What would happen if we turned the notion around? "I don't get even, I get mad."

That seems to be more faithful to Jesus' teaching. If you have something against your sister or brother, go and settle your account, then come and lay your gifts at the altar. Confronting someone or something is much more positive than revenge. There are always alternatives; they may not seem immediately apparent, but remember that God knows of your needs and Christ continues to intercede on your behalf.

Merciful God, you tame the tumult and can still the raging storm. Surround us during our times of trial and keep us from lashing out at the forces that oppress us. Help us to seek resolution rather than revenge and give us a measure of compassion to match our combativeness. Lead us by the light of your love for us, embolden us to speak the truth that can dispel misunderstanding, illuminate options that can cure conflict within us, and grant us courage through your indwelling Spirit.

Mark 6:30-46　　　　**Third Week: Thursday**

CARE-GIVING

The feeding of the five thousand is one of the best-known passages in the Bible. It's a phenomenal picnic! You wouldn't think that five loaves and two fish could feed so many. Yet the numbers weren't the important thing. What mattered was that "they all ate and were satisfied." Jesus saw to it throughout his entire ministry that persons were cared for and their needs were met.

The honeybee, next to the ant, is probably the most sophisticated of all insects. The beehive has a definite economy, with each member assigned a particular task. When you consider that a healthy hive will hold upward of ten thousand bees, that is a pretty highly ordered civilization.

Within the hive the division of labor is quite remarkable. The newly emerged worker bees are assigned care-giving responsibilities. Not yet strong enough to fly great distances, they feed the larvae and tend to the queen's needs. They clean the hive and act as air conditioners; by the beat of their wings they keep the hive at a constant temperature regardless of the weather outside. They receive the nectar and pollen from the arriving field bees and see to it that both are properly stored.

The field bees are the more mature bees. Their task is to fly out from the hive for up to two miles in search of nectar and pollen. They will forage among the fields and flowers in pursuit of their goal and, when laden, return to the hive. A bee in its lifetime will gather enough nectar to make one teaspoon of honey (remember that the next time you spoon honey onto your biscuit or muffin). If a field bee finds a particularly abundant source of nectar or pollen, she will communicate that to the hive upon her return. The hive then dispatches more field bees to the lucrative location.

Without field bees the hive would starve. It is a fact that a bee will actually work itself to death. From dawn to dusk the field bee makes as many flights as is necessary in order to accomplish its daily task. Depending on how near or far its field or endeavor happens to be, the number of round trips becomes impressive indeed.

Without the care-giving bees the hive would not function properly. The honeybee is a very fastidious insect. It literally cannot stand disorder or dirt in the hive. The care-givers are the nursemaids and the homemakers of the hive; they combine their talents to assure that the queen is well-kept, the infants are fed, and the hive is kept spotless.

Christian care means seeing to it that all are well-fed and satisfied. Each Christian has a unique talent and a corresponding task to perform. Care-giving begins by discovering what talents you possess and how you can best use those talents for the well-being of all. Some care-givers work outside the home. Their days are busy as they perform their assigned tasks, pollinating particular projects and cross-fertilizing their ideas with accomplishments. They attribute their work to their commitment to Christ; they seek to be faithful in whatever they do.

Other care-givers work inside the home. They nurture, manage, and care for the young. They see to it that the home is maintained and the environment is conducive to a balanced and coordinated daily schedule. They, too, attribute their work to their commitment to Christ and accomplish countless tasks daily in their quest for faithfulness. At home or outside it, Christians do care, and they seek to give of their talents for the well-being of all.

O God, you brood over all of creation and sustain it with your benevolent care. We give you thanks for Christ, the bread of life. Create within us the zeal to serve faithfully and energetically, to use well the talents with which you've endowed us, and to perform our tasks daily to your honor and glory. Make us tireless in our efforts to provide for our neighbors' well-being. Heighten our sensitivity to their needs and attune us to ways that we may serve them more faithfully.

EXPECTATIONS

Jesus walks on water; the disciples think they see a ghost; as many as touch him are healed. That's the way of the kingdom. Jesus calmed the terrified disciples and quieted the wind when they were on the water together. As soon as they landed, people thronged around him, hoping he would heal them. Whether on land or at sea, his ministry never ceased.

What to expect from the faith? The disciples found comfort when Jesus joined them in the boat, even though they were astounded by what he did. Jesus occasionally got weird looks even from those who were closest to him. The crowds expected great things from him, and those who touched him were cured of their afflictions. What can you expect as you journey in faith?

The first thing to expect is company. The Holy Spirit will be there as your constant companion. That means you'll never be lonely. Now, there is a difference between being alone and being lonely. Sometimes, people want to be alone. There is nothing wrong with that. They feel comfortable with themselves. Other people can't stand to be alone, because they have never gotten acquainted with themselves.

Those people may have a tendency to feel lonely and forsaken when there is no one around them. They can expect the company of God's Holy Spirit to help them feel more comfortable with themselves. A lot is written in the Bible about the Holy Spirit who hovers over you, who constantly watches out for you, who guides you and sometimes protects you. It is difficult to describe accurately just who the

Holy Spirit is or what the Spirit does. That's why there are so many descriptions for the Spirit that we can never say for sure. My favorites are those that describe the Spirit's presence as a gentle breeze or as leaves swaying in the wind, or those that call the Spirit a counselor or a constant companion. What they are trying to say is that the Spirit of God is present where you are, especially when you feel lonely, depressed, anxious, or sorrowful. During those times, be particularly watchful for the signs of a loving God who wants you to know just how much God cares. They will be there.

Second, expect an occasional weird look from people. You won't always fit in, because Christians don't always go along with the latest fads. We march to the beat of a different drummer, dare to be different, take our clues from the authority of scripture, have a vision of a higher order of priorities, and seek to live by those standards.

To be a Christian means to take positions someone won't like. There will be times when it does feel pretty lonely, when even those you thought were friends have forsaken you, when all you have, or hope you have, is the presence of the Holy Spirit to comfort you. People will gossip and say things about you to others. Even in the church, people sometimes don't treat other people very well.

Position yourself at those times to turn what could be a nasty situation into a positive one and show yourself to be above what others seek to demean. Above all, treat others with care and understanding. Often those who gossip are envious and yearn for some measure of the stature they see in you. Bend down to hear them and, yourself, help them to stand tall. Remember that with patience a weird look can turn into mutual admiration.

You still the storms of life, O God, and can turn the nights of our loneliness into the dawn of better days. You are the source of our comfort and hope, an ever-present strength in need. As Jesus comforted the disciples, surround us by your Spirit and give us peace. Help us to touch the hem of his garment and feel his healing power at work within us. Make our days worthy of the grace you give us and faithful in response to the ministry Christ calls us to perform.

Mark 7:1-23   Third Week: Saturday

HYPOCRISY

The Pharisees and Jesus argue about proper behavior. Does it mean eating with clean hands, hon-
oring human traditions, and concern about what to
eat, or has it to do with evil thoughts, deceit, envy,
slander, pride, and foolishness? Jesus was upset
when even his disciples failed to understand that
the latter were far more important than the former.
He taught them the fundamentals of godly behavior and was not too concerned about ritualistic
cleanliness.

Don Basilio sings a powerful aria about slander in
Rossini's *Barber of Seville.* Slander creeps around the
corners of life, hiding from the truth until it can find
receptive ears to enter. It then works its way into the
brain and infects the cells with its poison, consuming
human thoughts and intentions. Soon it reaches pro-
portions that can no longer be contained, and the
venom works its way to the mouth. There it erupts
over its intended victims. Charges spew forth that
malign character and damage relationships.

Jesus elsewhere in scripture had not too much
good to say about hypocrites. In the Sermon on the
Mount he admonished his followers not to follow
the example of those who gave alms ostentatiously
so that they would be praised by others. He also
cautioned against praying in public in order just to
be seen engaged in some pious acts. In Matthew 6:7
he warned against prayer that simply repeated
empty phrases because that was seemingly the religious thing to do. We know well how easy it is to see
the speck in our neighbor's eye but refuse to ac-
knowledge the log in our own.

In Greek drama, hypocrisy was wearing a mask in

order to hide one's true feelings or judgments; one could play the part of virtue and goodness without while seething with rage within. Slander occurs often when someone pretends a friendliness and concern for other people's well-being, only to accuse them, often unjustly, when their backs are turned.

Perhaps the saying is true that God was wise indeed to give us two ears and only one tongue. James wrote, "If any one thinks he is religious, and does not bridle his tongue but deceives his heart, this man's religion is vain" (James 1:26). Elsewhere he wrote of the tongue as "a little member" that "boasts of great things. How great a forest is set ablaze by a small fire!" (James 3:5). It can stain the whole body, set on fire the cycle of nature, so that "no human can tame the tongue—a restless evil, full of deadly poison" (James 3:8). That's quite an indictment, particularly when set over against the hymn by Charles Wesley, "O for a thousand tongues to sing our dear Redeemer's praise, the glories of our God and King, the triumphs of his grace!" James was right: With the tongue we bless the Lord and Father, and with it we curse our fellow human beings, who are made in the likeness of God.

Reinhold Niebuhr, in his book *Moral Man and Immoral Society,* noted how the dominant groups in society will indulge in the hypocrisy of claiming special intellectual fitness for the powers they exercise and the privileges they enjoy. They may claim moral superiority as well, and justify their superior advantages as fit reward for diligent and righteous lives. Niebuhr's point was that often nations will mask their motives of self-interest by appeals to moral principles.

All of which comes back to the point Jesus was making: It's not what goes into us that defiles us, but what comes out of us. Or James's comment about our tongues: Brothers and sisters, "this ought not to be so."

"O for a thousand tongues to sing our dear Redeemer's praise. . . . Jesus, the name that charms our fears, that bids our sorrows cease—Its music in the sinner's ears brings life, and health, and peace." Create a clean heart within us, O God, and restore a right spirit among us. Let not that which passes over our lips set ablaze what you create and hold dear. Curb our tongues of slander and deceit and loose them to proclaim your love.

FOURTH WEEK

John 6:27-40   Fourth Week: Sunday

HUNGER AND THIRST

Jesus admonishes his followers to seek the food which endures to eternal life. When they want from him some sign as to what that food might be, Jesus replies that he is the bread of life. The bread of God comes down from heaven and gives life to the world. Whoever comes to Jesus shall never hunger, and whoever believes in him shall never thirst. With that the disciples replied, "Lord, give us this bread always."

Hungering and thirsting are common metaphors in the Bible. During the wilderness wanderings, the Israelites yearned for the good old days in Egypt when they sat by the fleshpots and ate their fill. They felt Moses and Aaron had taken them into the wilderness to kill them with hunger (Ex. 16:3). Deuteronomy foretold how they would be humiliated before their enemies because of their disobedience; they would be naked, they would hunger and thirst, and they would be left without the things they needed (Deut. 28:48). Ezekiel foresaw the day when the Lord would care for the people: They would have "prosperous plantations" so that hunger would no longer consume them (Ezek. 34:29). The prodigal son finally came to his senses and asked himself why so many of his father's servants had bread enough to spare while he was perishing with hunger (Luke 15:17). To hunger was a sign of God's judgment; to be relieved from hunger was a sign of God's forgiveness and goodness.

The psalmist wrote how his soul thirsts for God as in "a dry and weary land" where there is no water (Ps. 63:1). Proverbs described how good news from a far country is "like cold water to a thirsty soul"

(Prov. 25:25). Jesus used the quenching of thirst as a sign of discipleship, "for I was thirsty and you gave me drink" (Matt. 25:35). And of course there is the Beatitude that says, "Blessed are those who hunger and thirst for righteousness, for they shall be satisfied" (Matt. 5:6). Jesus was consistent in his teaching that whoever comes to him shall never hunger, and whoever believes in him shall never thirst.

Today, there are still many in the land whose hunger and thirst are not just a figure of speech. Their hunger may continue to be a sign of God's judgment, not upon them but upon us who have been charged to carry on in Christ's name. It is we who are to offer the bread to the world to feed the hungry; our responsibility is to offer the cup of cold water as a sign of Christian responsibility. We have been called to be the stewards of the Lord's Table and serve all those who would believe in the Lord, Jesus Christ.

The metaphors of hunger and thirst continue to be a strong reminder to Christians today of just what their discipleship involves. The church has many agencies and programs seeking to alleviate world hunger. The church also advocates an end to the polluting of the world's waterways. Each one of us can support such programs and thereby assure their continuation.

Jesus would have all those who follow him hunger and thirst after righteousness. That is to say, no one of us should be content with our own present state of spiritual nourishment. For many of us in North America, hunger and thirst for food and drink is no problem. But too many of us are undernourished in our souls, whereas in countries less well off than we are, with our abundant supermarkets, many believers in Christ are well nourished in matters of faith.

Christ was concerned with the proper balance of nutrition for the total person. No one need hunger or thirst again, since he came as the bread of life. Let us offer that bread to the world, and ourselves seek the nourishment that will sustain our faith.

Giver of every good and perfect gift, we bring you tribute and glad praises. You water the earth and cause it to spring forth into blossom; you govern the seasons by which we live out our days. You nourish our longing hearts and quench our thirsty souls. We thank you for Jesus, the good news who brings new life. Hear our prayer of thanksgiving, and guide us toward renewed commitment. Help us sustain all those who call on us, as we offer the bread of life to the world.

BREAD

Shun the worship of idols! That's the word Paul sends to the Corinthian church. They don't need to worship anything or anyone except Christ. Why? Christ gave them all they would ever need: the bread of life, the cup of salvation, their freedom from inhibiting proscriptions, and their ability to love and care for their neighbor. They were bound together with Christ in a table fellowship that would sustain them and nourish them; Christ was indeed the bread of life.

Daniel Berrigan wrote in *Love, Love at the End* that when he heard bread breaking, he saw something else: "It seems as though God never meant us to do anything else. So beautiful a sound, the crust breaks up like manna and falls all over everything, and then we eat; bread gets inside humans" (Macmillan Co., 1971, p. 114). He speaks of bread as the "formal glory of God." Maybe it is. How could anything so basic to life do so much for humanity without being the formal glory of God? Maybe God didn't intend for us to do anything else than offer a crust of bread to our neighbor.

The Greek Orthodox church where I worshiped on the island of Crete had a wonderful custom. Someone in the parish baked the bread for the sacrament of the Lord's Supper. It arrived there in a large basket, sending out wonderful smells. From the many loaves the priest chose one for the Table. The rest were put aside; I wondered what happened to them. I found out after worship, when I left the church: The deacons were giving each of the worshipers a hunk of bread as traveling mercy on their way home. What a wonderful idea! Just suppose a family took that piece of bread and offered it to someone they chanced to meet who was really hungry. "Here, we have been fed the bread of life at the Lord's Table; now we offer you this bread that you too may have life." Wouldn't that be a wonderful way to extend the Lord's Table? Maybe God never meant us to do anything else.

Throughout history, bread has had a certain mystique. It is Shakespeare who in Hamlet (Act IV) has Ophelia refer to the baker's daughter who was turned into an owl for refusing bread to the Savior. In the German provinces, long ago, all bakers would avoid standing with their backs to the oven; it was an act of disrespect. In Romania today, if someone drops bread, he or she kisses it when they pick it up. In their *German Folk Tales* the Grimm Brothers tell the story of the child who died. As the mother was polishing and dressing the coffin, she decided to bake the child shoes of bread. The child was buried in these shoes, but the mother received no peace. It was only when the body was disinterred and proper shoes put on the child's feet did the soul remain quiet. There was nothing more precious to give the dead than bread; however, it was a sin to make the dead walk on it. For centuries it was preferable to set bread only on a tablecloth, so that the friend of humanity would have a soft bed. There are those today who will only break bread with their hands and never take a knife to cut it. The implication is that slicing a loaf is like putting a knife to the Savior. Such is the mystique that surrounds bread.

The next time you say the Lord's Prayer, know that to pray for daily bread is to ask God to provide all that is necessary for that day. Know also that as you offer bread to your neighbor you give all the love, acceptance, forgiveness, and suffering that go into caring for another person. God never meant us to do anything else.

Give us this day our daily bread, O God; support us all the day long. As the shadows lengthen may we know that what we accomplished was to your honor and glory. When evening comes let us abide in your peace which never fails. Throughout our days help us care for the hungry, the homeless, those who are healing, and those who are dying. May we extend our Lord's Table and invite in the strangers, that all who are gathered may taste the bread of new life.

Mark 8:1-10   Fourth Week: Tuesday

COMPASSION

Jesus has compassion on the crowds who follow him. Some have been with him for three days without anything to eat. He is afraid that they will be sent on their way hungry. Again the question arises: how to feed so many with such scant provisions? The way was found, however, since they ate and were satisfied. Jesus bade them farewell, got in a boat with his disciples, and was once again en route. He continued his trek as time and again the masses were healed, fed, and taught what it means to live in light of God's love.

Compassion is an intricately woven tapestry of emotions on behalf of another person. Compassion contains at least three important threads of life: sympathy, mercy, and beneficence. The first thread is sympathy. Sympathy is sharing God's concern for another person. Peter comes closest to describing the components of sympathy when he writes, "Finally, all of you, have unity of spirit, sympathy, love of the brethren, a tender heart and a humble mind" (1 Peter 3:8). Sympathy begins with that unity of spirit that puts people at ease with one another. Gone are attempts to belittle, begrudge, or denounce someone for whatever reasons. Instead there is a sense of being yoked in common sufferings, shared hopes, a mutual upbuilding, and a commitment to "withstanding" whatever occurs. In so doing, God's Spirit is likewise engaged and involved through the strength, the insight, the comfort, and the guidance the Spirit provides. So the first step toward compassion is to share with other persons God's concern for them.

A tender heart and a humble mind lead to the

mercy you extend to others. Like sympathy, mercy is also a God-like response; no, it is more of a God-inspired response. It is God who makes our hearts tender toward others. God breaks down those defenses we seek to erect so that others won't hurt us; God gives us the courage to reach out and extend ourselves to others without so much thought about what's in it for us; God helps us to identify those strengths we have to give and to recognize our weaknesses; God opens our hearts to feel what others are enduring.

Mercy is likewise the offspring of humble minds. Philippians reminds us how Jesus humbled himself and took the form of a servant (Phil. 2:7–8). Hebrews tells us how Jesus himself suffered, and was tempted as we are, and is therefore able to help those who experience similar temptations (Heb. 2:18). Jesus is our guide to humility and serves as our teacher in merciful behavior. As the Beatitudes state it, "Blessed are the merciful, for they shall obtain mercy" (Matt. 5:7). Humility begins with your willingness to serve others. From that will flow acts of mercy.

The third thread in the tapestry of compassion is beneficence. Beneficence consists of those specific acts of sympathy and mercy that come as results of unity of spirit, a tender heart, and a humble mind. By your deeds shall you be known! The best example of beneficence was the good Samaritan. He saw someone in need, and his heart went out to him. He went to him and bound up his wounds, pouring on oil and wine (Luke 10:29–37). That might have been enough, but it wasn't. He set him on his own beast, took him to an inn, paid a deposit on a room for him, and then promised to return and settle the full bill. Beneficence in that case was doing all that was possible, all that could specifically be accomplished to care for someone in need.

Today, put on compassion. Feel yourself clothed with a kindred spirit, a tender heart, and a humble mind. See how a little sympathy and mercy affect your neighbors and how an act of beneficence benefits them. Then you, too, will have draped them in the threads of compassion.

O Lord our God, by your wisdom you created us; we give you thanks for your benevolent care of us. We thank you for Jesus, who humbled himself on our behalf. We thank you for the Spirit, who yokes us with kindred souls. Open our hearts to their yearnings, and may we look with compassion upon them. Blend us through beneficent acts into a ministry whereby we become merciful and thereby receive a like portion of your mercy and grace.

SIGHT

Jesus again confronts the issue of hunger. This time the disciples were without bread on the boat ride across to the other side. He rehearsed with them the feeding of the five thousand and the feeding of the four thousand. Had they no sight to see what transpired? Then in Bethsaida a blind man was brought to him. Jesus spat and laid his hands on him. The blind man saw everything clearly.

Having newly arrived in the parish, I was introduced to one of the members, who immediately told me she was blind and could not see. In one of those rare occasions of Spirit-inspired responses, I quickly said, "Oh, but you do see, just differently from the way I do!" Well, that must have made an impact on her, because she told everyone what I had said. She could see. She identified people by their voices. She was aware of a person's presence. Through touch she could size up a situation quickly. She had developed her other senses to compensate for her visual impairment.

Sight, insight, hindsight, foresight, oversight: they all are ways we see things or fail to see things. Some people have a keen sense of insight. Call it the Spirit's guidance or intuition, they have the ability to put things in perspective. Hindsight has been claimed to clarify even the most perplexing problem. If only the gift of hindsight were immediately available, many of us would easily make crucial decisions. Foresight is a risky venture and one that many seek to practice and perfect. However, it is difficult to know what the variables will be, and so foresight is often not certain. We all commit oversight and sometimes pay dearly for it. Oversight can be corrected; it takes a reminder.

Many people have two other kinds of predominant vision. Some people focus quite narrowly; others concentrate on the periphery. Those who focus narrowly see what is immediately in front of them. There are those who would say they see only what they want to see. Theirs is a world of limited perspective, their horizon is bordered by the immediate present, and the insight of others they seldom entertain.

Other people are distracted by what occurs on the periphery; they find it difficult to concentrate on what is before them. They are, so to speak, always looking out of the corner of their eye. Call it suspicion, uncertainty, or even anxiety; whatever it is, they are often distracted by the edges of life.

A favorite exercise for youth groups is to take a "trust walk." Assigned in pairs, one of the two covers his or her eyes with cotton balls held in place by a bandanna. Each blindfolded person is then led by the seeing partner along a walk that involves touching the flowers, smelling the leaves, listening to the sounds around them, and tasting some mysterious foods. The walk teaches young people to focus on parts of creation they often don't experience when their eyes are open. Their reaction is almost always one of amazement. The lesson is intended to help them use all their senses in a way that opens the vast beauty of God's creation.

Learn to see things in a new way. Open your eyes to the world about you. As the television show *20/20* seeks to do, focus on something and try to see all sides. Use all your senses in such a way that you get the broad spectrum. As the hymn says, "Open my eyes, that I may see glimpses of truth thou hast for me; place in my hands the wonderful key that shall unclasp, and set me free."

"Silently now I wait for thee, ready, my God, thy will to see; open my eyes, illumine me, Spirit divine!" Open our ears, O God, that we may hear the voices of truth about us. Give us discernment to cast away falsehood. Open our mouths that we may proclaim thy love and broadcast afar thy redeeming grace and mercy. Open our hearts that we may enter into a kindred bond with our neighbors and shower upon them a measure of those same blessings thou dost amply bestow upon us.

Mark 8:27–9:1   **Fourth Week: Thursday**

DENIAL

Jesus asks the disciples who people thought he was. Some thought he was John the Baptist; others said Elijah. Jesus wanted to know what the disciples thought. Peter said he was the Christ, yet when it came time for Jesus to foretell his future, Peter rebuked him. But Jesus would stand for no misinterpretation or apprehension.

Peter wanted Jesus to be more than a fallen hero. Perhaps he sought a political figure who could dominate the current religious authorities. Maybe Peter was content with the wonder-worker who cleansed the people of demons and made them whole. Or was Peter quite content with Jesus as teacher? We are not told exactly what type of leader Peter thought Jesus to be. All we read is that when Peter confessed Jesus as the Christ, his interpretation of the Messiah was vastly different from what Jesus foretold.

Peter and Jesus confronted one another over Peter's misinterpretation. First, Peter rebuked Jesus; then Jesus did the same to him. Peter denied Jesus his forecast of death and subsequent resurrection. Jesus, in turn, denied Peter and accused him of being full of the devil. Then Jesus went on to teach the multitudes that those who would follow him must deny themselves. Within the short space of a few verses, three forms of denial occur: religious denial, parental denial, and self-denial.

Religious denial is perhaps the most common. Like Peter, people want to make Jesus conform to their image of what the Messiah should be. They too don't want to worship a fallen hero. They want someone who will enhance their own image. Idolatry rears its ugly head time and again, and Jesus will have none of it. The disciples are to prepare themselves for life in the Spirit, just as modern-day disciples need to conform to Christ's will for them. So, the first lesson is both to beware of the subtle ways we deny Christ and also not to create our own image of the Messiah.

Second, Peter must have been devastated when Jesus rebuked him. Parental denial leaves permanent scars when for some reason children don't measure up to their parents' expectations. Yet Jesus was patient with the disciples; he nurtured them, explained everything to them, supported them in all of their efforts, and constantly accompanied them. Only death would separate them from him. Parents have in Jesus a model of the care and compassion involved in guiding those in one's care toward responsible behavior. Jesus' rebuke was surrounded by empathy and was never intended as a denial of Peter's self-worth. The second lesson is not to deny to others the dignity God has vested in them.

Third, Jesus taught the multitudes that if they were to follow him they would need to deny themselves. When people are robbed of their self-worth it is difficult to deny whatever esteem they have left. Many of us just want to be accepted for who we are. We want to feel good about ourselves. Self-denial is easy for those who regard themselves as worthless. Yet Jesus would have none of that thinking either.

He wanted his followers to take responsibility for their actions. He would go to great extremes to give them new life. God loved them; Jesus surrounded them with his own life; they would henceforth live bathed in the eternal presence of God's cleansing Spirit. They would have life and that, indeed, abundantly. So what was there to deny? Deny the old self that is dead to sin and put on the new life, cared for and made whole in Christ.

Merciful God, you enfold us with the embrace of a caring and compassionate parent. We give you thanks for your abundant mercies. Hold us during times of trial, so that we do not waver in faith. Support us when we face decisions, so that we remain strong and committed to Christ. Help us to be the responsible children you want us to be, that at the end of the day we may hear the words, "Well done, good and faithful servant."

TRANSFIGURATION

Peter, James, and John accompany Jesus up a high mountain. He is transfigured before them; his garments become dazzling, better than any earthly bleach could do. Elijah and Moses are there to talk with Jesus. The whole scene is quite spectacular. Then the cloud appeared, and with it came the voice from heaven: "This is my beloved Son; listen to him." Jesus then set his sights on Jerusalem and beyond. All who would follow him were to heed his teachings.

Epiphany, transfiguration, and Pentecost have the same thing in common for me: Heaven and earth seem to come together for a time and set spectacular events in motion. They are in that sense a foretaste of what it will be like to be in the presence of the Almighty: the dazzling splendor, seeing the giants in the faith talking among themselves, the voice of God sending forth utterances. I'm afraid that, like Peter, I wouldn't know what to do. I'd probably make some feeble suggestion that in hindsight would seem like the dumbest thing I could have said. There he was, in the midst of greatness, and all he could think of was building shelters.

I had the good fortune of knowing the artist Corita Kent. Her art turned my world around. She had a way of taking bits and pieces of everyday, routine events and giving them a dazzling splendor that opened my eyes to new truths and wiser appreciation. Corita never engaged in small talk. Whenever I was with her I was always afraid I would say something that just wasn't appropriate. I was like Peter must have been. One year we were engaged in a project together, since she illustrated some books I wrote. One day she called and asked me what I meant by a phrase I had used, "God of the universe." An hour later I hung up the phone, completely drained of any further strength for that day. I had been in the presence of a person who for me brought heaven and earth together, and it had taken every bit of my being to be up to the occasion. Some people have that dazzling splendor.

All of us have our own high mountains, those special places where for a time heaven and earth come together. We go there to commune or to re-create, to find solace and comfort, to piece body and soul together. For me, Muir Woods in California has always held such reverence. Amid stately redwoods that dwarf me in size and whose age makes my accomplishments insignificant, there is a peace that passes over me. It is as though they invite me to walk among them for a while and to speak with them of what they have seen and all they have experienced. Regardless of what has been weighing heavily upon me, I always come out of the woods refreshed and inspired. Places may have that ability to transfigure us.

Events can also bring heaven and earth together. Many have found that sublimeness in the birth of their children. Others have found it while talking with an aged family member. I can listen to Vivaldi's *Gloria* and for a moment hear the angels singing. Time and again God has a way of breaking through the manic course of events we pursue and transforming the mundane into the sacred. For a moment our world stands still, transfixed in the presence of an awesome wonder, and God's time transforms the common into the sublime. No one can predict when or how such times occur. But like Peter, James, and John we come away convinced that we have truly been among noble company. Such are the traits of transfiguration.

"Mine eyes have seen the glory of the coming of the Lord." For that radiant vision we thank you, O God. For his transforming presence in our lives we praise you. As we behold your dazzling splendor through life's experiences, help us to be transfigured according to Christ's will. Take us and mold us into the creatures you would have us become. May we truly heed his voice and learn from him what it means to obey you. Send us forth from the mountain to serve you amid the valleys of life.

Mark 9:14-29   Fourth Week: Saturday

PRAYER, FASTING, AND ALMSGIVING

Only Jesus could drive the spirit out of the epileptic boy. The disciples tried and failed. When they ask him about it, he replies that only prayer has any effect on such spirits. Earlier Jesus had told the boy's father that all things were possible to those who believed. The scene emphasizes the fact that belief means more than just intellectual affirmation. It involves discipline, and three of the earliest were prayer, fasting, and almsgiving.

Prayer is that moment of honest encounter when we lay before God what he already knows weighs heavily upon us. Prayer begins best with thanksgiving for all God has done and continues to do in our lives. Thanksgiving also gives perspective to those burdens we presently carry. By rehearsing God's grace and mercy in the past, we are assured of his continuing faithfulness. As God has borne our anxiety and delivered unto us sufficient strength daily, we can rely upon God presently to hear our prayers.

Christ plays a significant role throughout our prayers. Christ intercedes on our behalf. Since Christ endured all forms of human suffering and now sits at God's right hand, we have in Christ a very present advocate. Christ knows of our needs and can rejoice with our successes and empathize with our needs. When we pray in Christ's name, we affirm over and over again our trust in that intercessory role Christ performs on our behalf.

The key to prayer is constancy. Paul writes that we are to "rejoice always, pray constantly, give thanks in all circumstances" (1 Thess. 5:16–18). That's good advice and a good formula to follow. To pray constantly is to become aware of the many ways God answers our prayers. They may not be the ways we would expect; they are God's ways, not our ways. God will hear us and we shall be shown the way as we come before God daily in prayer.

Fasting implies sacrifice. Often, during Lent, the practice was to give up something. Even today, I hear people say what they have given up for Lent. It is a noble practice, and usually what we abstain from we can easily do without. Fasting as a sacrifice sharpens the senses. It makes us aware of all we receive and also what we do with what we have. Fasting also makes us more compassionate toward those who view the option of fasting as a luxury. They are the ones who cannot decide to abstain, since abstinence for them is a forced life-style.

Fasting is a good way to put us in touch with the wilderness. As such it helps us to rely upon God's mercy, shorn for a time of all the comforts by which we seek to cushion our lives. Since for many of us the wilderness is not an easy location to reach, an occasional fast will help to bring the wilderness to us. Then it may be reassuring for us to be ministered unto for a time by the angels.

Almsgiving is another form of stewardship. Again, during days when we are besieged with requests from some charitable agency or another, it is difficult to get excited about almsgiving. However, a contemporary approach may be to assess how energy-efficient we are in our use of time, talent, and money. That is to say, Lent may be a good time to review our priorities and readjust our life-style accordingly. Otherwise, it is so easy to get caught up in the rapid pace of each day that very little time is taken for reflection on where we actually are going. Just as prayer begs for a moment daily, and fasting heightens our sensitivity, so almsgiving helps us to review how we are doing with what we've been given. All three are healthy disciplines.

○

All your works shall give thanks to you, O God, and all your saints shall praise you. Yours is the greatness, power, glory, splendor, and majesty; all that is in heaven and on earth belongs to you. Hear our prayers, O God, as we utter them, and bless our endeavors as we perform them. May we be drawn closer to the gates of your kingdom, there to behold your glory and receive afresh that commitment to follow you more faithfully throughout the course of our days.

FIFTH WEEK

John 8:46-59   **Fifth Week: Sunday**

STONES

The people have trouble with Jesus, particularly when he says, "If any one keeps my word, he will never taste death." What about Abraham? He died. What about the prophets? They died. Was Jesus greater than they? When Jesus said to them that he even preceded Abraham, that was more than they could take. They took up rocks to throw at him and caused him to hide and then flee.

This episode is the second such occasion in the eighth chapter of John when the people were about to stone someone. The first was when they accused a woman of adultery. In each case they were prohibited from accomplishing what they intended to do. With the woman, Jesus simply said, "Let the one who is without sin among you be the first to throw a stone at her" (v. 7). In the latter instance he himself escaped.

A friend of mine is a rock polisher. Wherever he goes he collects rocks. When he has a goodly assortment, he sets out his tumbler and fills the cylinder with these mementos, adds grit and water, and turns it on. After some days he will check the grit to see the progress. If it is time, he will drain off the old grit, add a medium type, and pour in the proper amount of water, and on it goes again. More days pass until the mixture is checked a third time. If the surface is ready, it is time to polish the stones. Notice how he differentiates between rocks and stones. To him rocks are to throw, stones are to polish.

At any rate he adds a fine polishing powder to the cylinder, and now it is time for the rocks to become polished stones. It is amazing what emerges. There are deeply colored veins, each stone producing its own unique identity. He can tell the geological formation and the different strata that caused the various designs the stone now reveals. When it was just a rock, all those data lay hidden beneath its nondescript crust. In the case of these stones, it took my friend first to care enough to collect them. Then he patiently tended them as he varied the mixtures in the grinding process. Finally came the crucial step when the rock was ready to become a beautiful stone. As the butterfly sheds its cocoon and enters the world a second time now colorfully adorned, so also these stones were this time much more than the rocks my friend found strewn along the side of the road.

I thought to myself, How often do we throw rocks rather than polish stones! It is often easier to judge someone on the spur of the moment than it is to take time and let that person's true beauty emerge. My friend knew just what grit to use and how much to add, but sometimes what we say rubs people the wrong way. If we took more time to learn their likes and dislikes, we would know what it takes to enhance rather than diminish their beauty.

It is often amazing what treasures there are beneath the surface. Everyone has a story. As with the stones, some take longer to emerge than others. Some people have rough surfaces for very good reasons. They have lacked the care to polish their fine edges. And, oh, what beauty breaks through that hard crust when for a time someone cares enough to listen! It is as though the pieces fall together and life is no longer so puzzling.

Rather than judging others prematurely or causing them to flee from the prospect of having rocks thrown at them, it would seem better if we were to concentrate on polishing stones. Polished stones will always have more beauty than thrown rocks.

Gracious God, this is the day which you have made; we will rejoice and be glad in it. Deliver us from those burdens that weigh heavily upon us. Give us this day the rest that will enable us throughout the week to serve you more faithfully. Open our ears to hear your word proclaimed, and let our mouths sing you praises. May our hearts be glad in the service to which Christ calls us, and may all that we do praise your holy name.

SERVANT

The scripture contains a trilogy of teachings: Jesus rehearses again his impending fate at the hands of the authorities; there is a discussion of true greatness and what it means to be a servant; the scene then shifts to those who were casting out demons in Jesus' name. If we were to summarize the teachings, it would be apparent that he was preparing his disciples for when he would no longer be with them. Emphasis was upon service, not some kind of status.

Mr. Rickard was a good friend of our family. He was a butler who had been brought from Scotland by some prominent family in San Francisco to serve their household. My parents had known his family in Scotland and retained their friendship with him throughout his years in the Bay Area. He was one of the proudest and most gifted people I knew as a child. He kept the family's cars immaculate; he knew how to cater a meal for five or fifty guests; his skills at carving were known throughout the city's social set, and he was forever in demand for some function or another; when he wove tales of his encounters with the rich and famous of that day, we youngsters were always eager to listen; then he would display his skill at carving as he deftly cut a roast of beef or a turkey down to manageable size to fit on our plates; nor did he stop there, for he also raised our consciousness as to the appropriate condiments to flavor each particular meat.

As I grew older I realized the source of Mr. Rickard's pride. He was not eager for status; those he served had more than enough. He just wanted to be known as one of the best at what he did. And what he did was serve other people very well. He was proud that during an evening's event he could anticipate the needs of the guests and be there to serve them before they beckoned. He was proud of the way he put the host and hostess at ease during a party, which allowed them to enjoy themselves and mingle with their guests. He was proud of his ability to complement a menu with the perfect beverage for a particular entrée, the appropriate array of food on a plate, the necessary service during each course, and the perfect ambience to satisfy the most impeccable taste. This was what being a servant meant to Mr. Rickard, and he was proud of his calling.

Jesus was not one to care much for status. The religious authorities had enough of that. He taught his disciples how much better it would be for them to be good servants. As such, they would have more than enough to do, and the care they provided their neighbors would be their reward. Today, we reward such care with tips. How often have you dined at a restaurant where the service was impeccable? There they have been, the waiters or waitresses and those who bused the tables. They never hovered but were always attentive. When your water glass was empty they quickly filled it; they never hurried you but cleared your place in a timely fashion for the next course. It was as though, throughout the meal, they kept an eye on you and were always attentive to your every need and desire. They too are proud of their calling, and our tip is a way of saying how much we appreciate their care.

Those who serve, whether professionally or voluntarily, are indeed the care-givers within society. However, they are not the only ones called to be servants. All of us are called by Christ to anticipate the needs of our neighbors and to be there to offer them a cup of cold water. "For truly, I say to you, whoever gives you a cup of water to drink . . . will by no means lose his reward" (Mark 9:41).

Merciful God, be gracious to us and hear us; make your face to shine upon us and bless us. You made your Son great among us; grant that we may become servants in his name. Help us rise above our need for recognition and the status that society confers. Let us find satisfaction in caring for neighbors and pride in the work to which Jesus calls us. May we offer hospitality to strangers and perhaps entertain angels unawares.

Mark 9:42-50   Fifth Week: Tuesday

SALT

Jesus took a dim view of sin. His attitude was that whatever caused it should be cast off. It would be better to live without the perpetrator than to face eternal damnation because of it. Salt is mentioned as the cleansing agent. However, if it has lost its salt-ness it won't be of much use. So he admonishes his hearers to have salt in themselves; then wounds can drain, healing occur, and they can live in peace and harmony.

You have heard it said that some people were "the salt of the earth." They had a certain stability, and not much bothered them. They were able to combine seriousness with humor without confusing what was appropriate. They were sensitive to other people's feelings and always made others comfortable in their presence. They were seldom judgmental, although they often used good judgment. There was an innate wisdom about them that people relied on and often sought.

Then you've also heard of "salty" characters, rough-cut gems most likely associated in some way with the briny deep. They had a coarse tongue, sometimes a vile temper, and seemed to live by and large just on this end of serious trouble. If they be-friended you there was nothing they wouldn't do for you. However, they were not likely the type you would choose to get close to.

Neither the salt of the earth nor the salty character could claim to be short on saltness. Both of them had it; they just expressed it differently. More often than not the salty character would rub salt on an open wound. It could be said that they were not often long on sympathy or compassion. Their coarsely ground nature was sometimes more abrasive than soothing. The salt of the earth were likely to be the opposite. They brought balm to troubled areas and would ease pain more than cause it. Healing just seemed to seep from their every pore.

What would it take to become a salty Christian? Jesus referred to his disciples as the salt of the earth and warned them against losing their saltness (Matt. 5:13). A salty Christian will enhance a situation, not dominate it. The secret of salt is to use it sparingly. Apply a pinch or two, and it will bring out the flavor in foods. Use it excessively, and soon salt is all one can taste. Salty Christians tend to bring out the best in others. They will complement another's gifts and talents, support them in their use of those talents, and help them refine their abilities for even greater capacity.

A salty Christian also enlivens a situation. Salt is likewise a leaven. "Enthusiasm" is a theological word that means "to be filled with God's Spirit." To enthuse is to be in God. Jesus warned the disciples not to lose their saltness. There is seldom anything worse than a bland witness. Those who go on a salt-free diet notice quickly how bland food tastes. To enliven a situation is to invite God's Spirit into your midst; it means to allow the leaven to permeate the gathering and allow it to come alive!

A salty Christian will not harden hearts. One of the negative features of salt is that excessive use hardens the arteries, constricts the blood's flow, and causes an increase in blood pressure. The heart must work harder than normal, and damage can result. Salty Christians are sensitive to excessive witness that can actually do more harm than good. Theirs is a tempered approach.

In Christ you are the salt of the earth. How well do you flavor whatever occurs? Enrich it with the stability, sensitivity, and good judgment Christ sought to evoke in all the disciples. Then others will see your good works and give God the glory!

Loving God, whose mercy is as fresh as the morning and whose grace sustains us throughout the day, enliven us with the refreshing gift of your Holy Spirit. Temper us by Christ's teachings and mold us to your will. Create in us a new heart fit for your service, and blend our desires with a taste of your wisdom. Let the salt within us add zest to daily life, and give us peace with our neighbors as Christ enlivens all that we do.

UNION

The Pharisees put Jesus to the test. The subject is divorce. Jesus refused to approach the subject negatively. Rather, he spoke of the creation, how God had created male and female, how they were to be joined together and become one, and how they were to complement one another in all they did. God created one flesh; they were man and woman. Each is less than whole without the other. Both are made one as they are joined together and live in harmony.

Much is written today about androgeny. Androgeny is the realization that there are uniquely feminine traits and uniquely masculine traits. Everyone has some of both; some people have more of one than the other. Rather than judging one kind superior, the emphasis today is to applaud both in a person and help enhance particular traits for the benefit of all. That is to say, women should not be judged because they have characteristics that are typically feminine. Nor should men consider themselves more worthy because they exhibit tendencies that are typically masculine.

Some women behave in masculine ways and assert themselves accordingly. Such behavior does not minimize their effectiveness, nor should they be considered less than women for doing so. There are men who have a nurturing side to their personality which could be labeled feminine. That does not make them less than other men; it may enhance their effectiveness. In fact there are some who say that each of us should recognize those traits that are characteristically other and develop them so as to enhance our total personality.

Union occurs when men and women can work

together in harmony. Jesus used marriage as the symbol of that harmony. Marriage is the joining together of two people in a blend of each other's strengths and weaknesses in a union that enhances both. You have known marriages where either one of the partners is less than whole without the other. In spite of their occasional differences or their idiosyncrasies, there is something about their being together that works for the common good. They form a team, with each one bringing to the table their opinions, desires, particular biases, dislikes, and even their ugliness. What emerges is a certain beauty and wholeness that complements both; their common bond enables them to be a team and to enhance their surroundings.

Now, while marriage may be the symbol for such unison, it need not be limited to the legal contract between a man and a woman. Paul likened our relationship with Christ to a marriage. Our union with Christ and the church is to be like that of a bride and a bridegroom. A "marriage" can occur in the workplace, among fraternal relationships, and within close associations as well. Marriage in those cases becomes the commitment to bond ourselves with another for the mutual benefit of all. It involves the commitment not to stereotype people according to presupposed traits that may limit them. Rather, it seeks to regard persons as integrated and diverse at the same time, the blending of which produces a unity that is more effective than the individual parts.

In that sense the union is like a symphony that emerges out of cacophony. Left alone, each of the instrumental sections may be incomplete and less than effective. Under the baton of the conductor, they are brought together and produce beautiful music. Jesus intended for life to have that kind of symphonic beauty. Each of us has our part to play.

Beloved God, Maker of heaven and earth, whosoever you have joined together let no one separate. Bind us together as men and women in the joint venture of life. Help us to become mutually supportive and upbuilding of one another. Let us be sensitive to those strengths and uniquenesses that set us apart, and to the need we have of one another that unites us. May we rejoice in our diversity and applaud our unity through the One who makes us whole, even the Christ.

Mark 10:17-31   Fifth Week: Thursday

TREASURES

The man with great possessions is crestfallen. He thought he obeyed all the commandments; in that sense eternal life was assured. However, Jesus told him to go and sell all he has, give to the poor, and then follow Jesus. The man went away sorrowful. Those who were rich would have difficulty gaining entrance into God's kingdom. It would, in fact, be easier for a camel to go through the eye of a needle. Treasures have a way of claiming allegiance that belongs only to Christ.

During my youth, there was a store not far from home called the Treasure Trove. Today, it would be similar to a flea market, only it was under one roof. What a delight it was to visit! There you could go and feast your eyes on treasures of all sizes, shapes, assortments, and categories. Depending on my mood, I could spend an hour among the comic books, visit the stamp and coin department, gaze at the clocks, pretend among the costumes, conjure up all kinds of tales about the origins of some of the memorabilia, or just leaf through the pages of some book. It was a trove, all right, something like four or five attics all gathered under one roof. Today, I wish I had bought some of the items; they would be worth a great deal more now.

That's the way it is with collectibles; they amass a certain value. For some people the value is historical. Particular ages continue to live in the pieces collected. For others their value is sentimental. Each time the piece is held or observed we remember the story involved in its acquisition. Some collect things for the challenge. The harder they are to find, the more rewarding the quest. Others accumulate in order to own a complete set. Anticipation mounts toward purchasing the final piece that will make your set whole.

"Where your treasure is, there will your heart be also" (Matt. 6:21). Professional collectors caution against accumulating any collectible only for its potential monetary value. There are better ways to make your money grow. They will advise you to collect for enjoyment and relaxation. In other words, don't make what you collect into a treasure that it may never become. Strangely enough, their advice sounds similar to what Jesus told the rich man.

Probably a reason I liked the Treasure Trove so much was that I couldn't afford to put a monetary value on any of the items it contained. For one thing, I had no money to purchase them, and for another, I had no sense of their worth. They were there just for me to explore, imagine, recall, and dream about. In that sense, they were a source of enjoyment and relaxation. "Do not lay up for yourselves treasures on earth, where moth and rust consume and where thieves break in and steal" (Matt. 6:19). The problem with treasures on earth is that they may be consumed, broken, or stolen. People may become unduly concerned and spend more time fretting about them than actually enjoying them. At that point they have begun to control us and are no longer in the proper perspective. Jesus sought to have his followers avoid this kind of idolatry. Riches could not save anyone. They provided no freedom and eventually could consume their owner.

Jesus wanted his disciples to be free to follow him, to grow in the faith, to go where they were needed. We also need to shed whatever baggage hinders our effectiveness on behalf of that same Gospel. While treasures may be meaningful and troves fun to explore, let us unburden ourselves of idols so that our ultimate allegiance is to Christ alone.

You alone are God, and we find in you all we will ever need for salvation. Only in Christ can we enter into your kingdom, and we give thanks that he has called us to share in his triumph. Guide us during our journey, that we may be faithful; help us avoid temptations that could lead us astray. Keep us from compounding our sin by seeking false treasures. Help us to rely solely on Christ, our Redeemer and Friend.

Mark 10:32-45   Fifth Week: Friday

BAPTISM

James and John, the sons of Zebedee, ask if they may sit at either side of Jesus in his glory. He responds that such a request is not his to grant. However, they could drink from the cup of which he was to drink, and they would be baptized with the baptism he received. Some of the disciples were indignant that James and John would even make such a request. Jesus said again that whoever would be great must be a servant, and whoever would be first must be the slave of all.

Three basic questions are asked of parents when they bring their children for baptism. First, do they reaffirm their faith in Jesus Christ as Lord and Savior? That is, do they commit themselves anew to wage battle against the principalities and powers that vie for our attention? We constantly hear the question: What are your priorities?

That Jesus is Lord means that we seek to live by his example. We have chosen among the myriad of options his teachings and commandments as God's will for us. Jesus first called us and we chose to follow him. If need be, we would lay down our lives for his sake. We do that, in fact, each time we pray "not my will, but thine, O Lord."

He is our Savior. There is nothing we will ever endure that he has not already suffered on our behalf. He goes before us as the pathfinder. He not only charts our course but serves as a guide to what to avoid. He knows the divergent paths we might take and has shown in history how he will seek the aimless and lost. When our earthly work is done, he will be there to welcome us as we cross into eternal life.

Second, do you claim God's covenant promise on

your children's behalf, and do you look in faith to the Lord Jesus Christ for their salvation as you do your own? To claim the covenant promise is to join the mighty throng who throughout history traced their lineage back to Abraham. Together, we are now linked with sisters and brothers—Asians, Indians, Orthodox, Africans, Hispanics, Reformed, Free Church, all who shared the same baptism and partook of Christ's cleansing rite.

To claim that covenant promise is to exercise the act of inheritance. You bequeath to those who will follow a legacy that accompanies their birthright, the legacy of the name of Christ. As with most inheritances, it will be up to the children to decide what they will do with it. For the time being, they have received one of their first bequests, the opportunity to grow up in Christ and themselves inherit the kingdom of heaven.

Third, do you now, in humble reliance upon God's grace, promise to set before your children an example of the new life in Christ, and do you promise to pray with and for them and to bring them up in the knowledge and love of God? That question has three functions: the prophetic, the priestly, and the pedagogical, or teaching, function.

The prophetic function is to set an example. The major and minor prophets by example foretold God's will for the Israelites. Jesus sought by example to show the disciples how to respond to God's will. Paul used his life as an example of the new life in Christ and the freedom found in the gospel.

The priestly function in the Reformed tradition belongs to all of us. We all have the right and the responsibility to pray on behalf of one another. Through our prayers we intercede on behalf of God's people everywhere.

The teaching function occurs as we join together

in Christ's household to nurture each other for greater maturity in Christ. Baptism marks the initiation into the salvation journey. Through example, intercession, and instruction we join the throng who received the baptism by which Jesus was baptized.

Source of all we have and are, you sent Christ to save us. Washed clean of our sins, we can humbly approach you and give you all praise. You clothe us in the robes of our baptism; you name us and set us apart. Help us to serve as examples for those about us as we intercede on their behalf. Give us wisdom to learn your will for us, curiosity to seek your truth, and a nurturing nature to help others grow in the admonition of Christ.

Mark 10:46-52   Fifth Week: Saturday

WELL-BEING

Bartimaeus, the blind beggar, calls out for Jesus to have mercy upon him. Many who are there rebuke him, but their threats do not thwart his desire to be cured. He perseveres until Jesus notices him and requests his disciples to bring the man to him. When Jesus asked what he wanted, Bartimaeus replied, "I want to see again!" Bartimaeus received his sight. Jesus sent him away well, his faith had been so great.

All of us want to be well. We want to feel good, be content with how we look, proud of our achievements. We like to receive recognition for our accomplishments; we don't want to be hindered from doing what we want to do. Bartimaeus, in that sense, was just like everyone else.

He saw in Jesus the opportunity for well-being. After all, Jesus' fame had spread through the countryside; he was known for his cures and miracles. It was worth a chance. So Bartimaeus called out for Jesus to have mercy on him. Why the crowds rebuked him for doing this, we're not told. Maybe they didn't want him to disturb Jesus, or they may have thought he was unworthy, or insignificant, since he was a beggar. At any rate, their rebuke only made him more persistent.

He got Jesus' attention. The disciples told Bartimaeus to take heart, Jesus was calling him. With that, the man sprang up and went to Jesus. Presumably, Bartimaeus expected at that moment to be made well. When Jesus asked him what he wanted, he replied that he wanted to see. There wasn't any hesitation. He had pursued what he sought and was not going to waver in his conviction that Jesus could heal him.

The result was that he immediately received his sight. He then joined the band following Jesus. Bartimaeus gives us some clues to well-being. The first is desire. Bartimaeus desired that Jesus have mercy on him. He was not content with his condition; he wanted a change. He showed no signs of resignation, of being able to go on sitting by the roadside while Jesus passed. Rather, Jesus provided an opportunity for Bartimaeus to change his condition; he acted on his conviction and sought Jesus' mercy.

Second, Bartimaeus was tenacious. He would take rebuke from no one. He must have thought himself as worthy of Jesus' mercy as the next person. Or his desire was great enough to ward off his attackers. He persisted in his approach to get Jesus' attention despite the odds. His tenacity paid off.

Third, there was his faith. Bartimaeus must have believed in Jesus' abilities. Nothing within the text indicates that he had any doubts. If he could just have an audience with the Master he could be made well again. Jesus noticed his faith and commented on it. As was the case with many of Jesus' cures, we are told that it was his faith that made Bartimaeus well.

Fourth, Bartimaeus became a follower. He had not just used Jesus for his own desires. His commitment was deeper than that. His faith was such that after he became well he would continue to be faithful. We do not hear more from him or about him, so anything said would only be conjecture. But his faith was such that he followed the Christ.

Well-being begins with a desire for change. Tenacity helps, because the way may be difficult. With faith comes hope and confidence that the quest will be successful. The commitment to follow leads to patience and perseverance. To believe in Christ is to know that God has gone to great lengths to make you well. In that sense, like Bartimaeus, your faith can make you whole.

Blessed are those whose strength is in you, O God. You bring hope to the afflicted, strength to the lame, and healing to all who are estranged. Through Christ, who sits at your right hand, you hear our needs before we utter them. Bend your ear to our prayers and surround us with your all-embracing arms. Bear us throughout times of distress and trouble, and give us strength sufficient for all that this day may bring.

HOLY WEEK

Zechariah 9:9-12   **Palm/Passion Sunday**

PEACE

Zechariah's vision is the humble entry of one who will bring peace to the nations. Because of God's covenant the captives will be freed. Dominion will extend to the ends of the earth. Hope will be restored. It will be a time when armaments of war are cut off, and there is anticipation of triumph and peace. So rejoice greatly, people of God, and shout aloud, O sons and daughters. God's herald comes to bring peace to the nations!

Humility, freedom, being at home with all of God's people, and hope: These are four primary ingredients of peace. Jesus humbly entered Jerusalem. The fanfare that initially surrounded him quickly dissipated as he was charged, tried, and eventually condemned. Throughout his ministry he never sought to call attention to himself. Rather, he practiced what he taught his followers, obedience to God and humble service to all those in need.

Humility is a trait that frees us from calling attention to ourselves. Gone is the drive to justify our every action. We are freed, in humbly accepting God's love and care for us, to offer that same kind of benevolence and hospitality to our neighbors. As James wrote, "Humble yourselves before the Lord and he will exalt you" (James 4:10). Humility is the trust that God will care for our needs daily; indeed, God does so each time we humbly confess our sins. In Christ we learn of our pardon and stand exalted and worthy of God's grace.

Jesus' sacrifice on our behalf broke once and for all the power that sin and death have had over us. He would endure God's trial of all nations, their rebellion, their greed, their disobedience, and their warfare against one another. Jesus would take the burden of God's wrath upon his own shoulders as he bore the cross. Thanks to him, there would henceforth be nothing that could separate us from God's love. With that assurance we can then confess our sins daily to God and gain the peace that comes with the assurance that in Christ God accepts us in spite of ourselves.

In this sense we are bound together with all of God's people everywhere. "If we love one another, God abides in us and his love is perfected in us" (1 John 4:12). The great quest for Christians around the world is to break down the walls of hostility that separate us. Our common baptism calls us to learn of one another's cultures, customs, and beliefs, that we may truly celebrate our unity amid our diversity. The time is at hand for the church universal to bind itself in closer harmony so that it can begin to form a united front on perplexing issues. That quest begins with each one of us as we commit ourselves to learn of others around the globe.

The hope is for the day when all of God's people will dwell together in harmony. In Jesus Christ, God has come to earth to give us life, abundant life. Our vision is of the day when all the earth can breathe a sigh of relief. The forest will laugh outrageously, and the birds of the air and the beasts of the fields will join for a moment in a chord that can be heard all the way to heaven. All humankind will be transformed into a kaleidoscope of colors, blends, and mixes, creating life in a myriad of fashions. The heavenly hosts will be summoned to begin setting up for the great festive banquet. Jesus is coming home, and he is bringing a crowd with him for supper. And the choir of angels will be heard rehearsing their alleluia chorus, for what God started will be complete once and for all. Then God will say, "Amen!"

Bringer of peace to the nations, we give you thanks for Jesus Christ, the herald of good tidings. We confess that our warfare is not ended and that estrangement divides us. Forgive us for hostility that still breeds distrust. Help us to be reconciled with our neighbors, to work toward the release of the captives, and to treasure the hope that all the world will dwell in unity. Let us, in all we do, truly become those agents of reconciliation that Christ called us to be.

PRAYER

Jesus gets angry with those who were using the temple to transact business. In his opinion, they were desecrating the house of prayer. He then teaches the disciples some facts about faith. One of the facts had to do with prayer. Prayer requires belief that whatever one prays for will occur. Another is that as soon as you pray for it, it is already yours. A third is to use prayer to forgive others their trespasses against you.

There are basically three obstacles to prayer: doubt, impatience, and selfishness. Remove any one of them and your prayer life will become more rewarding. The first obstacle is doubt. People often have difficulty believing that what they pray for will actually occur. Some people, in fact, are surprised when their prayers are answered. Whether in the past their prayers went unanswered or were answered in unexpected ways, people have been disappointed in the response to their prayers. Doubt has also arisen because of the insincerity of the prayer. There are those who use prayer as a wish list, sometimes to get things otherwise unobtainable, at other times to get out of uncomfortable situations. In those cases, the people thought it would be nice if their prayers were answered, but they doubted it would happen.

To remove doubt as to the efficacy of the prayer is to make the prayer more genuine. To believe with all your heart that such-and-such will be answered is to reorder your own priorities. You will yourself exert some energy toward its attainment. Prayer in that case will be something you really desire. So to remove doubt is to put the subject and the object of the prayer in tune with one another. That is bound to affect its effectiveness.

Second, get rid of your impatience. Patience is a discipline we learn by practice. Patience takes trust and perseverance. Patience means we must allow whatever forces are involved to have time to work. Patience is not easy within a culture that is fed a diet of heat-and-serve. Jesus said, "Whatever you ask in prayer, believe that you have received it, and it will be yours" (Mark 11:24). Patience is the willingness to engage in the process as well as waiting for the final product.

To believe you have already received that for which you prayed is to trust that God will provide for you daily all you need to sustain you. Day by day you shall then move toward the goal of your prayers. The end may not be in sight right away; the quest may take perseverance. Yet each step of the way you shall be led. What you receive will be God's will at that time and place as you patiently pursue the course of your prayer.

Third, many prayers blind us to the needs of others, particularly those that only focus on our desires and needs. Jesus said that each time we prayed we were to forgive anything we might have against someone; then God would forgive us our own trespasses. To seek to remove selfishness from our prayers makes us more aware of others' needs. At the same time, our prayers for them put our blessings in perspective. It becomes more difficult always to pray for ourselves when we see how much others really need.

To forgive anything we might have against someone makes us more likely to work on their behalf. The result is that our prayers become less self-oriented and more neighbor-oriented. Eventually, we will give thanks for the countless blessings God gives

us, intercede on our neighbor's behalf, pray for forgiveness for sins committed, and ask God to grant us
strength daily, so that all we do may give God glory
and honor.

*Merciful God, you stoop to hear the faintest whisper. Give ear
to our prayer and receive our thanksgiving. We bless your name
for the day you give us, for the peace that envelops us throughout
the night, for strength and health with which we can follow your
will. Abide with us as we pursue our tasks; may all we do bless
your holy name. Frustrate our acts that hinder your kingdom,
and enhance all we do in accordance with your will.*

Mark 11:27-33   Holy Week: Tuesday

AUTHORITY

The question that Jesus confronted time and again was, By what authority do you do what you do? Once again, this time in the temple at Jerusalem, the chief priests, scribes, and elders want to know the source of his authority. Jesus is quick to answer their question by asking another: Was John's baptism from heaven or from men? When his antagonists hedged on their response and said they did not know, Jesus felt no necessity to divulge the source of his authority.

Have you ever had the feeling that some things were better left for others to say than to say them yourself? For example, that you are humble. We can genuinely be suspicious of people who call themselves humble. Yet if another person says that someone is humble, that's different. Pride is another example. For someone to say "You should be proud" has an entirely different connotation from saying of yourself, "I should be proud" of a certain accomplishment.

There are characteristics that are best left for others to mention rather than for you to boast of them yourself. Authority is one of these. Again, I get somewhat suspicious of people who claim to have authority. It's a different matter if they then go on to cite their source of authority. In that sense they are no longer claiming themselves as its origin. However, if they stop short of describing the source, then their claim to authority, like humility and pride, seems to have less creditable roots.

In the text for today, as in other examples throughout Mark's Gospel, Jesus never claimed to have authority unto himself alone. The closest he came to citing his own authority was in Mark 2:10, where we read, "But that you may know that the Son of man has authority on earth to forgive sins." In that case, Jesus did not say that he, Jesus, had authority unto himself. He used a title that would indicate just the opposite: namely, that he was vested with a title that carried authority with it. Elsewhere, we read that Jesus taught them "as one who had authority" (Mark 1:22); that was Mark's opinion. In Mark 1:27 the crowd was amazed because Jesus commanded the unclean spirits with authority. In Mark 3:15 Jesus gave the disciples authority to cast out demons, and similarly in 6:7 he gave them authority to cast out unclean spirits. In the text for today he refused to disclose his source of authority. He never claimed to have that authority unto himself alone.

It is best to consider authority as an endowment. Something or someone has endowed you with it, and you now have it as a servant of that particular office or person. In that sense, authority is a calling. It carries with it certain responsibilities. Up to a certain age, parents have authority over their children. Their responsibility is to care for and nurture their children until they can assume responsibility for their own lives. Little by little the parents will endow them with more and more authority to make their own decisions.

Authority can be misused. It can be used as a sign of grandeur or to bolster someone as being greater than someone else. Some people may even hide behind it. Jesus would have none of those misguided approaches. He sought to make clear that his authority came from God alone. His charge was to use the authority he'd been given to bring all people closer to God's intent for their lives. Authority is always best used when it serves the intentions of those who grant it.

It is good to sing your praises, O God, and give you thanks for all your gifts. You endow us daily with your mercy; you forgive our sins. We dwell as a family within Christ's household; because of your grace we are saved. Help us to use wisely those talents you give us; keep us humble and free of self-grandeur. May we look to you for authority as we seek to serve others. Make us worthy stewards as we care for all of creation.

BLESSED

Jesus sends two of his disciples into the village to find a colt for him to ride as he enters Jerusalem. When the disciples return, he sits on the colt and the procession begins. Those who line the route spread their garments on the road, and others spread branches. It is a triumphal entry, and cries are heard: "Blessed is he who comes in the name of the Lord! Blessed is the kingdom of our father David that is coming!"

Elliott Wright, in his book *Holy Company,* writes, "The Christian's promised land is God; the route to the goal is the way of holiness, a path not smooth—and Christians hobble, too. Halting, faltering, even saints trip, but Jesus Christ, who leads the way, who is the way, does not. Those following 'The Way,' as Christianity was first called, 'dare to walk strongly' through the rough" (Macmillan Co., 1980; p. 1). Jesus guided the throng along the way to Jerusalem. Thereafter many would hobble with halting and faltering steps. Even the saints would trip. But Jesus who led the way would not. In spite of the fate that awaited him, the punishment he would endure, his steps would be firm and his course prescribed.

For the moment the crowds called him blessed. It was an accolade he was willing to share with the world. Those poor in spirit would inherit the kingdom of heaven. For them life itself would be self-effacing, free from worldly things and all claims to self-sufficiency. They would put on Christ, seek to live in Christ, and through the grace of Christ dwell in the promise of life everlasting.

Those who mourn would be comforted. As Wright reminds us, "mourners are powerfully, righteously

upset over the strength of sin and evil" (p. 51). They
hurt when their neighbors hurt. They are mourners,
not moaners. They will seek to cure the ills of a
sin-sick world. God, in turn, will comfort them
throughout their quest.

The gentle will be blessed, for they shall inherit
the earth. Tamed by God's love, they shall seek to
change the way people think and act. As for themselves, they are unafraid to offer their own ignorance
and weakness to God, who can transform it into
wisdom and strength.

Those who hunger and thirst for righteousness
shall be blessed, for they shall be satisfied. Their
appetites whetted by Christ, who came to set the
creation right, they will strive in all they do to bring
reconciliation and peace. Their satisfaction will come
when Jesus is truly the way, the truth, and the life.

Blessed are the merciful, for they shall receive
mercy. Knowing God's grace and forgiveness, they
will be the first to break down whatever barriers
divide neighbors. "Therefore lift your drooping
hands and strengthen your weak knees, and make
straight paths for your feet, so that what is lame may
not be put out of joint but rather be healed" (Heb.
12:12–13).

The pure in heart will be blessed, for they shall see
God. Bathed in the love of God and washed clean of
their sins through Christ's reconciling sacrifice, they
shall live their baptism, guided by the Holy Spirit.
The Spirit will guide them, caress them, cajole them,
and correct their ways as they seek to conform to
God's will for them.

Those who make peace will be blessed, for they
shall be called the children of God. The vision of
shalom goes ever before us as a guiding beacon amid
the turbulent shoals. Although the way may be
rough, those who seek peace will always work to-

ward the absence of war, an end to hostilities, right relations with God, and personal serenity.

Finally, those who are persecuted for the sake of righteousness shall be blessed, for the kingdom of heaven is theirs. Although many of us will never become martyrs, we shall remember always those who have gone before us. They have shown us the way, finished their work on earth, and now abide eternally with God. They are the hosts of heaven who with all those who are blessed will gather at the table for the great heavenly banquet.

Blessing and honor and glory and power be unto you, O God most high. You are the God of deliverance who brought the Israelites out of Egypt. You raised Christ from the cross and he now sits at your right hand, there to intercede on our behalf. You have sustained us throughout this Lenten season. Now prepare us to dine with Christ, that we may receive new life and look forward to the day of his resurrection.

Mark 14:12-25   **Maundy Thursday**

BASIN AND TOWEL

Jesus sends two of his disciples in search of a man carrying a jar of water. When this man entered a house they were to say to him, "The Teacher says, 'Where is my guest room, where I am to eat the passover with my disciples?' " The disciples found the man, and when evening came they assembled for the meal. There Jesus took the bread and the cup, but not before he predicted that one of the disciples would betray him.

In Jewish history, water was the sign of life. Cities were built around wells. Moses quenched the Israelites' thirst. The psalmist sang eloquently of still waters that restored the soul. It could be said that Jesus was fixing that history in his disciples' minds. Henceforth, his ministry, even on the night of his betrayal, would be marked by a pot of water from which flows a mighty stream to refresh and renew the world.

Mark wrote no further about the householder's significance but went right into the evening's events. John, however, picked up on the theme and developed the significance of water as a sign of renewal. John writes that after Jesus had eaten the passover meal with his disciples, he girded himself with a towel, poured water into a basin, and began to wash the disciples' feet. When he had finished he said to them, "If I then, your Lord and Teacher, have washed your feet, you also ought to wash one another's feet" (John 13:14).

Since then the basin and towel have become symbols of Christian discipleship. That is to say, what Mark started with the figure of a man carrying a jar of water, John finished with the symbol of the basin and towel. Water was used by Jesus not only as a sign of refreshment but also as a sign of renewal. As the man carrying a jar of water became a sign of the times, the basin and towel became a sign of commitment.

The basin and towel in that sense also become a logical extension of baptism. Since we are baptized into Christ and the water is a symbol of cleansing, the disciples in turn are to cleanse one another. The extension of our baptism is to show the same care and compassion for our neighbors that Jesus showed for his. The basin in that sense becomes an extension of the baptismal font. The basin is a symbol of taking the font, which contains the waters of baptism, and carrying those waters out into the midst of society. The towel is likewise girded about us as a symbol of our new status as Christ's disciples. We are the stewards of this water of renewal, called to refresh the weary travelers along their pilgrimage through life, and caretakers of the creation entrusted to us.

Holy God, in Christ you poured out your love on behalf of all creation; we come with thanksgiving and praise. As the bread is broken, restore us to a right relation with our sisters and brothers. As the cup is passed, renew a right spirit within us. Keep us from denying Christ daily or barring from the table those who hunger and thirst. Help us to offer the stranger a cup of cold water and thereby care for others as Christ taught us to do.

John 13:36-38   Good Friday

NO

Peter wanted to know where Jesus was going. Jesus told him that where he was going Peter could not follow him. Peter pressed the point to the extent that he vowed he would lay down his life for Jesus. Jesus then confronted him with the reality that the cock would not crow before Peter would have denied him three times. History proved Jesus' words to be true.

"No" conjures up the worst kind of images: Doors slam in our faces; an angry or forceful parent says "no"; someone turns their back on a loved one; a relationship is severed with no hope of reconciliation; a lover betrays a mate; society refuses to believe that atrocities occur; a dying patient gives up all hope of a possible cure. Why was Good Friday necessary? What was its purpose? Was it the means by which believers could heap all their guilt on the one they called "Teacher" and then send him out to be slaughtered at the hands of the mob?

Some people have admitted that they have a harder time believing in Easter than they do Good Friday. Sin makes more sense to them than salvation. After all, they know they are guilty; they themselves deny Christ daily. How can God forgive them so easily when they find it hard even to forgive themselves? In that sense "no" is a part of everyday living. Some use it to protect themselves; others are afraid of commitment. To believe takes time and effort, whereas "no" is simple and definite.

Was Good Friday God's "no" and Easter God's "yes"? Maybe God had to slam the door once and for all on the forces that hindered God's will from occurring. God as the angry parent said "no" to the sin that was rampant. If it would take Jesus Christ to sacrifice his own life in order to overcome sin and its power, then so be it! God would never turn away from humankind. In fact, Good Friday would bring alive the possibility of reconciliation. Without saying "no" to sin, to the forces of evil, even to Jesus' earthly ministry, there would be no hope of affirming Christ's eternal presence.

Peter's "no" was symptomatic of human irony. As Paul wrote to the church at Rome, "I do not do the good I want, but the evil I do not want is what I do" (Rom. 7:19). Humankind has never been able to save itself; it will turn its back on the good that can redeem it and follow the course that leads to its own destruction. Peter misunderstood Jesus' intentions in departing. When Jesus was gone Peter felt betrayed and denied him. In so doing, Peter turned his back on his only means of salvation and chose instead to think he knew better than Jesus what Jesus should do.

Building on the work of Elisabeth Kübler-Ross, we can add to her description of the stages we go through when we lose a loved one: denial, anger, bargaining, depression, acceptance—and hope. Peter was perhaps at the first stage of the process. He may have then passed through the others. We do know from Acts 3 that he accepted the risen Christ and performed a significant ministry on Christ's behalf. The beauty of Good Friday is that God delivered Jesus Christ as the hope of the world on the day of resurrection. We can therefore rest assured that, in spite of our "no," God will likewise deliver those who put their faith in this Christ, accept him as their Lord and Savior, and abide in him as the hope of the world.

"Abide with me: fast falls the eventide; the darkness deepens; Lord, with me abide! When other helpers fail and comforts flee,

Help of the helpless, O abide with me." Let us not depart from you, O God, though the way be hard, the journey long. Help us to endure the cross with the faith that sustains us through perilous times, the hope that abides, and the love with which Christ first loved us.

COMPLETE

The author of Hebrews writes about God's rest and how we should strive to enter that rest. On the seventh day after the work of creation, God rested. The creation was complete and it was good. Today is the day not to harden your hearts, since there remains a Sabbath rest for God's people. We now have a great High Priest who is able to sympathize with our weaknesses. We may with confidence draw near to the throne of grace. There we shall find mercy and grace to sustain us in time of need.

Think of God's work as completed but not yet finished. You will then be close to what the author of Hebrews was writing. From God's point of view, everything was complete from the foundation of the world. God could pronounce it good and rest. But from our point of view the creation was not yet finished. God would not rest until humankind believed and obeyed. So in a sense we live in the midst of ambiguity. Things are not as they should be, although everything was in place when it was created.

Now Jesus Christ has come to help us bridge the gap between the complete but not yet finished. In that sense he has been called the author and the finisher of our faith. In him we may find the rest the author of Hebrews wrote about. Through him we may with confidence approach the throne of grace. Because of him we can catch a glimpse of what the finished product will look like. "The wolf shall dwell with the lamb, and the leopard shall lie down with the kid, and the calf and the lion and the fatling together, and a little child shall lead them" (Isa. 11:6).

In another sense, Lent is complete but it is not finished. Lent is complete as a season. We have endured the time of discipline, of introspection, of our own experience with the wilderness and whatever sacrifices we've suffered. However, the work of Lent is not finished until we take what we have endured and apply what we've learned to every day of our lives. Lent would be less than fulfilled if people just returned to the way things were as though Lent never occurred. We can finish Lent as we discipline ourselves to live more faithfully and obediently throughout the year.

Then what we have endured and learned will be complete but not finished until we put that faith and obedience into practice with our neighbors. Just as our lives have been touched by the Holy Spirit, so also can we touch the lives of others. The author of Hebrews wrote that as we approach the throne of grace we may receive mercy and find grace to help in time of need. That same mercy and grace we are now to extend to other people.

We will offer them grace when we let them know that we accept them as the complete creatures God created them to be. We won't seek to remake them in our own image or think any the less of them when they don't conform to our ways. We will strive to enhance who they are with all their strengths and weaknesses and help them in all ways to feel good about themselves.

We will show them mercy as we join hand in hand with them through our common pilgrimage. Then we will sense it when they are frightened, we can lift them when they fall, we can uphold them when they are slipping, and comfort them when they mourn. For in the end we know that we shall dance with them when all our earthly work is finished.

Great Architect of the universe, you fashioned us according to your will. You molded us and breathed the breath of life into us. You made us to live in harmony with all your creation. We bow down before you and give you all praise. Honor us now with your presence, that we may with confidence approach your throne of grace. Endow us with mercy, that we may be the faithful and obedient persons you created us to be. Let us find in Christ the Author and Finisher of our faith.

EASTER

Luke 24:13-35   Easter Sunday

THE COMPANION

While two of Jesus' followers are on the road to Emmaus, Jesus approaches them, but they do not recognize him. They recount what has happened and how their hopes have been shattered. After Jesus interpreted for them the events' significance, they invited him to stay and dine with them. When Jesus broke the bread their eyes were opened. They went immediately to tell the disciples, who confirmed the fact: "The Lord has risen indeed!"

Alfred North Whitehead characterized all religion as "a transition from God the void to God the enemy and from God the enemy to God the companion" (*Religion in the Making*, Macmillan Co., 1927, pp. 16–17). Along the Emmaus road God became the companion. Jesus' followers were undoubtedly perplexed by the events that had occurred. Jesus of Nazareth had indeed been a "prophet mighty in word and deed before God and the people." His subsequent death shattered their dreams. God had in Jesus appeared so real to them, and now the void had once again enclosed them. All this and more they related to their traveling companion, who listened intently. Finally he interpreted to them the scriptures concerning himself.

All of us at some time in life make that "transition from God the void to God the enemy and from God the enemy to God the companion." Not long ago one of the young women in a communicants class read a letter she had written to God. Her reason for writing was for God to be present to her in some tangible form. God was still the great unknown, even though she so desperately wanted to believe. She wanted God for a companion rather than a void.

Others in the parish have confessed during counseling their anger at God. Because of some self-doubt or pervasive anxiety and resulting depression, they have sought relief through prayer. What they've encountered was not immediate answers but sustained silence. So they have come seeking answers because they were angry with God. One of the parishioners told me that he still was not over the counsel his pastor gave him when his first child died. The pastor, probably out of his own need to find answers to life's perplexing questions, told my friend that God needed his child more than he did. At that my friend replied, "Well, God be damned!" and stormed out of the church.

Self-doubt, anxiety, depression, and the quest for answers often lead to anger. But, like the Emmaus road experience, it is often during those lowest moments of life that God the enemy becomes God the companion; when the stranger comes and listens to our heartfelt tales of longing and provides an embracing comfort that has heretofore been unavailable. It is then that anxiety turns into a feeling of serenity, joy occurs out of depression, hope emerges from hopelessness. Healing begins to happen and good is once more returned for evil, forgiveness replaces retaliation, and courage triumphs over fear.

We learn through such circumstances to recognize that stranger as the living Lord. And there comes a time when, with Paul, we can admit that nothing in all creation "will be able to separate us from the love of God in Christ Jesus our Lord" (Rom. 8:39). Yes, Christ is risen indeed! When Jesus appeared to the disciples, they were startled and frightened. They thought they had seen a ghost. But he soon dispelled their fears with a simple request: Did they have something for him to eat? Since then, Jesus Christ has become our companion around the table and elsewhere, an ever-present help in time of need.

Glorious God, this is indeed the day which you have made, a day of gladness and rejoicing. You cause new life to burst forth with great beauty and fragrance. You adorn the creation with splendor and grandeur. We lift our voices to sing you praises. Help us to walk henceforth in the confidence of Christ's company and look forward to the day when we will dine with him in glory. Surround us now with the assurance of your Holy Spirit as we sing, Alleluia, Christ is risen indeed!

INDEX OF SCRIPTURE READINGS

Exodus
16:3............ 99

Deuteronomy
28:48.......... 99

Psalms
63:1............ 99

Proverbs
25:25....... 99–100

Isaiah
11:6........... 164

Ezekiel
34:29........... 99
39:21-29........ 23

Zechariah
9:9-12......... 147

Matthew
5:6............ 100
5:7............ 106
5:13........... 130
6:7............. 93
6:19........... 136
6:21........... 136
11:28.......... 46
11:28-29........ 21
13:33........... 58
25:35.......... 100

Mark
1:1-13........... 30
1:14-28........ 33
1:22........... 154
1:27........... 154
1:29-45........ 36
2:1-12.......... 39
2:10........... 154
2:23–3:6 45
3:15........... 154
4:1-20.......... 60
4:21-34........ 63
4:35-41........ 66
5:1-20.......... 69
5:21-43........ 78
6:1-13.......... 81
6:7............ 154
6:14-29........ 84
6:30-46........ 87
6:47-56........ 90
7:1-23.......... 93
8:1-10......... 105
8:11-26........ 108
8:27–9:1 111
9:2-13......... 114
9:14-29.... 117
9:30-41........ 126
9:41.......... 128
9:42-50........ 129
10:1-16........ 132
10:17-31....... 135
10:32-45....... 138
10:46-52....... 141

11:1-11........ 156
11:12-25...... 150
11:24.......... 151
11:27-33...... 153
14:12-25....... 159

Luke
10:29-37...... 106
15:17.......... 99
24:13-35....... 169

John
5:19-24......... 51
5:24........... 75
5:25-29........ 75
6:27-40......... 99
7:24........... 76
8:7............ 123
8:46-59........ 123
10:30.......... 52
13:14........ 159
13:36-38....... 161

Acts
ch. 3.......... 162

Romans
3:27........... 51
5:4-5.......... 18
7:19........... 162
8:39.......... 170
14:10.......... 76

1 Corinthians
1:31......... 51–52
3:16-23......... 42
4:8-20.......... 54
5:1-8........... 57
10:14–11:1..... 102

Galatians
6:2............. 21

Philippians
2:7-8.......... 106
3:12-21......... 19
3:14........... 20

3:16........... 20
4:1-9.......... 21

1 Thessalonians
5:16-18....... 117

Hebrews
2:10-18........ 27
2:18.......... 106
4:1-16........ 164
11:1........... 67
12:1-2......... 27
12:1-14........ 17
12:12-13....... 157

James
1:26........... 94
2:24........... 52
3:5............. 94
3:8............. 94
4:10.......... 147

1 Peter
3:8........... 105

1 John
4:12.......... 148
4:20........... 52